Light a Candle for the Feast of Flames

One thing that candles do, in a season dark and cold, is to serve as tiny reminders of the greater light and life-giving warmth that comes from the sun.

For those who live in the northern hemisphere, the festival of flames comes while winter's grip is still upon the land. Once this part of the year was called Wolf-month or Dead-month. Today we call it Candlemas, Imbolg, or by other names. For many of our ancestors, snow covered the sleeping earth, the nights were still long, and the gaiety of the solstice holidays had long since faded. Food supplies were beginning to look scanty and moldy, and the promise of spring seemed far away. And yet—the people celebrated.

In the cold darkness, they found reason for hope: a gust of wind less chill, a few minutes more of gray daylight, a solitary crocus pushing through the snow. They created a holy day, a festival, a feast—and under many different names, it is with us today.

About the Authors

Amber K joined the Temple of the Pagan Way in Chicago, receiving her initiation and ordination there. She has worked with Circle, New Earth Circle, and The Pool of Bast, and helped found the Coven of Our Lady of the Woods (OLW). She has served as Publications Officer and National First Officer of the Covenant of the Goddess, and taught in the Cella (priestess) training program of RCG, a national Dianic network. Her son, Starfire, is a Wiccan security officer.

Azrael Arynn K brings to the Craft her experience as a police officer, race car driver, stockbroker, and architectural designer, as well as a doctorate in law. She is a talented costume designer and ritualist. Both Amber and Azrael are third-degree priestesses in the Ladywood Tradition of Wicca. They met at a Wicca 101 sponsored by Our Lady of the Woods in 1992 and were handfasted in 1994.

The authors have taught many workshops at Pagan festivals and conferences, including Pantheacon, Heartland, UEA, Dragonfest, Florida Samhain Pagan Gathering, Starwood, and others. They are part of the team launching Ardantane, an inter-traditional Wiccan seminary to be based near Santa Fe. (For information, write to the Ardantane Project, c/o OLW, P.O. Box 1107, Los Alamos, NM 87544, or see the web site at www.Ladywoods.org or www.Ardantane.org.)

Amber and Azrael live in Los Alamos, New Mexico. Their home doubles as the OLW covenstead.

To Write to the Authors

If you wish to contact the authors or would like more information about this book, please write to the authors in care of Llewellyn Worldwide and we will forward your request. Both the authors and publisher appreciate hearing from you and learning of your enjoyment of this book and how it has helped you. Llewellyn Worldwide cannot guarantee that every letter written to the authors can be answered, but all will be forwarded. Please write to:

Amber K and Azrael Arynn K
c/o Llewellyn Worldwide
P.O. Box 64383, Dept. 0-7387-0079-7
St. Paul, MN 55164-0383, U.S.A.

Please enclose a self-addressed stamped envelope for reply, or $1.00 to cover costs.
If outside U.S.A., enclose international postal reply coupon.

Many of Llewellyn's authors have websites with additional information
and resources. For more information, please visit our website at www.llewellyn.com.

Brigit's Festival of Light and Life

Candlemas
Feast of Flames

Amber K and Azrael Arynn K

2001
Llewellyn Publications
St. Paul, Minnesota, 55164-0383 U.S.A.

FIRST EDITION
First Printing, 2001

Book design and editing by Connie Hill
Cover design by Lisa Novak
Cover painting by Hrana Janto
Interior illustrations by Carrie Westfall
Quoted passages on pp. 15 and 17 (footnotes 27, 30) reproduced from *Festivals Together -
A Guide to Multicultural Celebration* by Sue Fitzjohn, Minda Weston & Judy Large,
ISBN 1869890469, Hawthorn Press, Stroud, Britain.www.hawthornpress.com.
Available in US from AP - (800) 856 8664'

Library of Congress Cataloging-in-Publication Data
K, Amber, 1947–
    Candlemas : feast of flames / Amber K & Azrael Arynn K — 1st ed.
        p.   cm.
    Includes bibliographical references and index.
    ISBN 0-7387-0079-7
        1. Candlemas.   2. Brigid, of Ireland, Saint, ca. 453-ca. 524.   3. Brigit (Celtic deity).
4. February—Folklore.   I. Title: At head of title: Brigid's festival of light & life.   II. K, Azrael
Arynn, 1955–   III. Title.

GT4995.C36 K36 2001
394.261 — dc21   2001038897

Llewellyn Publications
A Division of Llewellyn Worldwide, Ltd.
P.O. Box 64383, Dept. 0-7387-0079-7
St. Paul, MN 55164-0383, U.S.A.
www.llewellyn.com

 Printed in the United States of America on recycled paper

Dedication

We dedicate this book with love to

Maxine Lois Lester Randall

Who, like the goddess Brigit, loves poetry;
And like Saint Brigid, loves kindness and compassion;
And like both, is a beautiful blonde.

And to Tess Erwin

If the rest of your life was anything like your cornbread—
I REALLY wish I'd known you.

Amber K and Azrael Arynn K
(aka Kitty and Elizabeth)

Other Books by Amber K

True Magick (Llewellyn Publications, 1990)

Moonrise: Welcome to Dianic Wicca
(Reformed Congregation of the Goddess, 1992)

Pagan Kids Activity Book (Horned Owl, 1986, 1998)

Covencraft (Llewellyn Publications, 1998)

Preámbulo a la magia (Llewellyn Publications, 1999)

Contents

Contents

Contents

Acknowledgments

We want to thank the following people who made this work possible or at least helped immensely:

The hard-working folks at Llewellyn, especially Nancy Mostad and Connie Hill;

Our immensely talented covenmates who have created many superb Imbolg or Candlemas rituals, from which we have borrowed with thanks; and especially Tehom, for her editorial suggestions; and Cernos, for shoveling the walk, bringing pizza, and other moral support throughout the creative process;

Aunt Faye, who tried my high-altitude scones and declared them perfect without changes for sea level.

Thank you all!

Amber and Azrael

Terminology and Grammar

We do not believe in the "generic masculine" (the sexist notion that "he" refers to people of both sexes) and have tried to avoid it. Unfortunately, it is awkward to include both genders in every sentence, such as "He or she is fortunate if he or she can find a ready-made Imbolg robe that fits him or her." Instead, we have often used "they" and "their" to indicate the indeterminate singular as well as the plural. For example, "If a participant wants to make a Brigid's Cross, they should begin by gathering straw or rushes." We know perfectly well that this is ungrammatical by conservative standards, but it is becoming increasingly commonplace in actual usage—and it's not sexist.

The Authors

Introduction

This is a book about celebration; specifically, celebrating the ancient seasonal holiday that happens about February 1 and 2, and is known as Candlemas, Imbolg, Brigit's Eve, Lá Fhéile Bríd, and by a host of other names. Along the way we will explore other February holidays, old and new, such as the Roman Lupercalia, Valentine's Day, and the Chinese New Year. We will meet an extraordinary lady, goddess or saint, who personifies the spirit of the season; like the holiday, she has many names: Brigid, Bride, Brede, Brigit, Brigantia, and more.

Candlemas has always been very special to us. It is a celebration of hope: the light returns, the darkness retreats, the promise of spring is offered. It is a time of purification; for many villages and nomadic clans of past times, this meant enforced fasting because food was scarce. For modern people who do not face the threat of starvation, it is still a time of physical and spiritual cleansing in preparation for the new year's challenges. Many Pagans and Witches also choose this time to clean and reconsecrate their ritual tools.

The ancient Romans celebrated in ways that may seem odd to us, such as chasing around the city streets and whipping one another with goatskin thongs. Even here, however, the theme of purification appears, since this ceremonial flagellation was intended as a kind of spiritual cleansing.

For the pastoral Celts, it was the breeding season when ewes swelled with new life. This was vital because their flocks were their livelihood, their source of food and clothing, their real wealth.

For other peoples of northern Europe, the day was sacred to Brigit, the triple goddess of inspiration and poetry, smithcraft, and healing. For

Christians, it became Candlemas, the day when candles (representing the return-ing light) were blessed in the church; and also the Feast of the Purification of the Virgin, and on top of that, the Feast Day of Saint Brigid.

To many, this holy day is also a time of initiation and personal transformation. Initiation means different things to different people, but most agree that it is an event or ritual that marks an individual's entry into a new role (such as adulthood, priesthood, or membership in a secret society) or into a higher state of conscious-ness or spiritual development.

What better time to mark these important transitions than the first celebration of the change from winter into spring . . . the festival of returning light . . . and a time which has for centuries been devoted to cleansing and purification?

Whatever the symbolism and functions of this holy day, the timing seems per-fect for anyone who has to cope with long and severe winters. The Winter Solstice holidays are long past; the food supplies (for our ancestors) may have been stale, monotonous, and shrinking; the cold, wet weather seems as though it will go on forever; summer seems like a distant fantasy. At this time more than any other, we need a reminder that warmth, light, and life will return; that at the darkest hours in human affairs, there is always hope. In the words of Albert Camus, "In the midst of winter, I found within myself an invincible summer." Perhaps that is the true meaning of this holy day.

In this book, we offer the customs and traditions of the festival, delicious recipes old and new, and ceremonies and rituals (designed for solitary celebrants, families, and groups) to help you to mark the event. We present several divinato-ry methods for those who want a glimpse into the future, and all kinds of ideas for house-cleaning—not only your home, but YOU: mind, body, and spirit.

This book has no plot, because it is not that kind of tale, but the cast of charac-ters is diverse and wonderful. Here you will encounter a Chinese dragon who turns the Wheel of the Year, the lady who shared Saint Brigid's bed at the abbey of Kildare, and an insightful groundhog named Punxatawney Phil. Here are gods and goddesses, blacksmiths and kings, bishops and Druids, fawning dogs and clever foxes, who will inform and entertain you.

The book is written from a Pagan perspective; however, we hope that it is also enjoyable to our Christian friends and to anyone who likes celebrating the holidays, even and especially the holiday that falls at this dark and cold time of the year. You don't have to be any particular religious faith to look forward to spring, and to like a good party!

Writing this has been frustrating and fun; usually more of the latter. Amber took the lead in researching Brigit, and has come to know her—in a complex, multi-layered way. "At first she was a figure of mythology," says Amber, "rather remote and abstract. Then, reading about the Saint, she became a historical person—distant, but warm-blooded and more real. The barriers of time and my own preconceptions gradually faded, until I could almost reach out and touch her."

Azrael has taken the primary role in designing the feast, researching the creation of candles and their magickal uses, and writing about divination appropriate to the theme and season. Finding ancient recipes and making them palatable to moderns has been a challenge, especially given the fact that we live at an altitude about 7,000 feet higher than the people of the British Isles. "The craziest part of creating the feast, once I had decided to have authentic foods from three time periods," says Azrael, "was sorting out which foods were actually available in the British Isles before the Crusades."

We hope you like reading this book. More importantly, we hope you use the book. Work with Brigit, organize the rituals with your family and friends, use the recipes (and eat the results), make the fancy candles, cleanse your life, and make ready for the light and warmth of spring. Reading is delightful; but the secret of life is in the doing.

Blessed be,
Amber K and Azrael Arynn K
Los Alamos, New Mexico
June, 2001

The Festivals
of February

In the northern hemisphere, this festival comes while winter's grip is still upon the land. Today we call it Candlemas, Imbolg, or by other names. Once this part of the year was called the Wolf-month, or Dead-month. For many of our ancestors, snow covered the sleeping earth, the nights were still long, and the gaiety of the solstice holidays had long since faded. Food supplies were beginning to look scanty and moldy, and the promise of spring seemed far away. And yet—they celebrated. In the cold darkness, they found reason for hope: a gust of wind less chill, a few minutes more of gray daylight, a solitary crocus pushing through the snow. They created a holy day, a festival, a feast; and under many different names it is with us today.

The festival has been called Imbolg and Oimelc, the Feast Day of Saint Brigid, Candlemas, Lá Fhéile Bríd, and by names spoken in the mists of prehistory, but lost today. There is an overlapping complex of holy days in Europe, clustered around the first to the third of February; and several other related festivals later in the month. We will explore several of these special events, beginning with the days when humanity's hold on survival seemed tenuous at best.

The Ice Ages and the End of Winter

If winter is an inconvenience for some people now, it was a serious challenge to our medieval ancestors. And to our still more distant ancestors, it was a gamble with death every single year.

Imagine the Paleolithic era—the Old Stone Age. Imagine it not from our perspective, as a dim prequel to civilization with its abundant food, central heating, and vast transportation networks. Imagine being there, and there is . . . all there is.

Winter, on the vast steppes of Asia. For a thousand miles in any direction there is nothing to break the force of the frigid wind. Gray skies, glaciers far to the north, grass brown and sere where the endless wind has stripped away the snow. There are seventeen in your clan, since your grandmother died. She was forty-one, an ancient Crone, and could no longer keep up with the migration. Now the clan follows the tracks of a herd of musk oxen, hoping for food.

That night you camp in the lee of a low mound, and the people chew on the last dried strips of mammoth meat from a kill made weeks ago. The hunters ranging ahead have not caught sight of the musk oxen, and their tracks may be erased by morning. The wind howls like the spirits of the lonely dead, and there is a current of fear and hopelessness among the living. More than one clansman expects to join his ancestors soon.

The shaman stands. She is a little young for her position, but was the closest thing to an apprentice old Nev had, before he died last fall of the coughing sickness. She speaks: "The Moon has passed through Her cycle once and more, since we marked the Longest Night. You all know this. But the nights still seem long, and food is scarce. You wonder if the winter will ever end, if warmth will ever return to the land. Now I say this: I have measured the length of the nights, as Nev taught me, and they are shorter. The daylight grows. This is the message of the Great Mother, Her promise that spring will come! She sends another message;

I have dreamed it. Within two days we shall find the herd, and as much meat as we can carry. So pass around what is left of the mammoth meat; eat what you wish, for more is coming. Trust the Mother!"

She speaks with authority for one of fourteen summers. The people believe, and soon the last of the food is shared out among the clan, and they dance around the hot, leaping flames of the bone-fire they have built.

The Bear Goddess of Neolithic Europe

One of the oldest forms of the Goddess is that of the bear, and one of the earliest recorded holy days of February honors Her in that form, perhaps because the awakening of hibernating animals is one sure sign of spring's approach. According to Marija Gimbutas, a scholar of Old European deities, "The concept of the goddess in bear shape was deeply ingrained in mythical thought through the millennia and survives in contemporary Crete as 'Virgin Mary of the Bear.' In the cave of Acrotiri near ancient Kydonia, a festival in honour of Panagia (Mary) Arkoudiotissa ('she of the bear') is celebrated on the second day of February."[1]

The bear was apparently a central figure in the Paleolithic religions of Old Europe and Asia. The hundreds of bear-headed clay figurines found at archaeological sites in Eastern Europe seem to represent the primal mother-goddess; some are seated on thrones and decorated with lunar crescents. Female bears are known for their fierce devotion to their young, and so the bear was a symbol of motherhood.[2] As the bear protects her cubs, so the bear-goddess protects the tribes by bringing spring with her emergence from winter's sleep.

Bears are also connected with water; bear-shaped vases of early European cultures are covered with zigzags, chevrons, and striated diamonds, all patterns symbolic of flowing water. The themes of water and fire appear again and again in connection with end-of winter celebrations; fire for warmth against the cold, water thawing from ice and snow as spring returns.

The Eleusinian Mysteries of Greece

Let us move ahead thousands of years to another spring festival, in which the Goddess has divided into a more human Mother and Her returning Daughter. In ancient Greece, the lesser Eleusinian Mysteries were celebrated at the end of January and beginning of February. This festival commemorated the return of Persephone from the Underworld to her mother Demeter. Demeter, as you may recall, was a Mother Goddess who brought life to the world, and made the crops grow and the bees give honey. When her daughter Persephone was stolen away (or eloped, in some versions of the story) to the Land of the Dead with the god Hades, Demeter mourned, life slipped from the land, and the first winter came.

A compromise arranged by the gods allowed Persephone to reign as Queen of the Underworld for half of each year, and return to the world of the living for half. When she returns, bringing the spring, the goddess Hekate and the spirits of the dead chosen for rebirth accompany her.

The Greeks held a great celebration to mark the occasion. First there was a torchlight procession, in which the participants combed the land and even waded into the sea, recreating the search for Demeter's lost daughter. When word came that Persephone was found, the assemblage cheered and held a great feast to celebrate.

Lupercalia

The Romans regarded February as a time of cleansing and purification—*Februarius mensis,* "the month of ritual purification." However, fertility and love were also popular themes. Several festivals were celebrated, but their biggest event was the Lupercalia on February 15. This holiday was named for the *Lupercal,* the grotto where the infants Romulus and Remus came ashore after floating down the Tiber

River in a basket. There they were suckled and raised by a wolf, and later grew up to found the city and nation of Rome. Why was the sacred bear of ancient Europe largely replaced by the wolf in classical Rome? Edain McCoy believes that "Lupercalia celebrated the beginning of the wolves' mating season. . . . Wolves mate for life and their union was seen not only as a sign of spring, but of the eternal union of the Goddess and her Sun God."[3]

In part, the festival of Lupercalia honored Faunus (also called Lupercus), a goat-footed god of Nature, flocks, crops and gardens, music, animals, and much more. Goats were sacrificed to him, and then his priests took to the streets wearing goatskin loincloths. They were known as the *Luperci* (the priests, not their loincloths.) Each carried goatskin thongs and their role was to hit everyone they saw; presumably this token scourging was a symbolic ritual purification.

Married women received a bonus effect, however; the thongs supposedly encouraged fertility. Technically, the Luperci were supposed to strike them gently across the palms, but apparently some women were so serious about the fertility issue that they stripped naked to encourage the Luperci to go further.

The younger people celebrated by putting the names of willing girls into a jar; the boys would draw names and discover who were to be their partners for the festivities. This custom spread and was still popular in England and Scotland hundreds of years later.

Pope Gelasius I, who reigned over the Roman Church from 492–6 C.E., "banned this cheerfully scandalous festival and met with such an outcry that he had to apologize."[4] In 496 the feast of Lupercalia was changed to the feast of Saint Valentine, and instead of girls' names, the names of various saints were put into a box for people to draw out. Prayers would be offered to the saint you drew.[5] We can only guess how wildly popular this change was with young people. Oddly enough, the custom seems to have evaporated over the years.

The Roman Church was finally able to officially abolish Lupercalia, although its replacement was never quite as respectable as the Church fathers might have hoped.

The Lupercalia was definitely *the* social event of the season; however, the Greeks and Romans were not stingy with their festivals. A citizen who didn't have to work for a living could spend the entire month preparing for holy days, celebrating them, or recovering from them. Here is a sampling of the Roman and Greek holidays for the month:

January 31 to February 2: Februalia dedicated to Vesta, "The Shining One," goddess of fire and the hearth.

February 2: The day honoring Juno Februata as the virgin mother of Mars.

February 6: Festival of Aphrodite, Greek goddess of love, beauty, creation, vegetation and flowers; known to the Romans as Venus.

February 7 to 9: Feast of the Old Greek, Roman and Slavic goddess Artemis/Diana/Diwitsa, as creatrix, midwife of birthing creatures of all kinds, protector of the young, and punisher of child abusers.

February 12: Festival of Diana as protectress of wildlife; she was also a Triple Goddess of the Moon, Virgin, Mother, and Huntress.

February 14: Feast of Juno, Queen of the Heavens, consort of Jupiter, Great Mother, goddess of Earth and the moon, protectress of women.

February 15: She's back! Festival of Love for Aphrodite.

February 16: Celebration of Victoria, goddess of victory.

February 26: Day of Hygeia, goddess of health and healing.

February 27: Day of Selene, the Mother aspect of the moon goddess, patroness of magick, intuition, fecundity, and the tides of the ocean.

Each of these deities had other major festivals as well; these are simply their holy days that happened to be in February.

The Celts and Imbolg

Further north, the Celtic peoples marked the season in their own way. Imagine yourself in an ancient Irish village: the solstice is past, the days are dreary, the memory of warmth seems like a fading dream, and the promise of spring is scarcely to be seen. It is then, "Late in January, as the Wolf Moon wanes or the Chaste Moon waxes to full, we begin to prepare for the Imbolc Sabbat."[6]

Many of the Celtic peoples were pastoral herders, making their living from their flocks of sheep. Naturally enough, their seasonal festivals reflected their livelihood. One of the major Celtic festivals was Imbolg (or Imbolc), pronounced "em-bowl/g" or "im*mol*'g," (with a tiny hesitation or unstressed vowel after the "l"). Imbolg means "in the belly" and refers specifically to the pregnancy of the sheep, and more broadly to Mother Earth quickening with new life.

A second name for this holiday is Oimelc ("oy-melk"), meaning "ewe's milk," since the ewes were lactating for their new lambs. A folk verse from the Isle of Man makes oblique reference to the abundant milk, calling the holiday "White Brigid's Day." Milk was not simply for the lambs, or a nice beverage for people to drink with their cookies, but an important part of the family's nourishment. Because it was precious, it was worthy of the gods; so an offering of milk might be left out overnight, or poured out on the threshold or the ground, as a libation to thank the goddess and encourage still more bounty.

Imbolg is also considered one of the four great Celtic fire festivals, "but here the emphasis is on light rather than heat, the strengthening spark of light beginning to pierce the gloom of Winter."[7] The days technically begin to lengthen at Yule, the Winter Solstice, but by Imbolg we can clearly see the change. Truly the sun's light is with us longer each day. This is the first harbinger of spring, our assurance that the Wheel is turning and the long, warm days of summer will return. The Scots celebrate the growing light not only with Imbolg but also with *Up-Kelly-Aa*, a fire festival on January 28 that honors the sun goddess.

It is a busy time of year, and the air is filled with anticipation. Housewives check the family pantry and root cellar, hoping that enough food remains to feed the family through the spring; in the barn, the farmer casts a practiced eye over his hay and grain—it's a long way yet to the harvest! But with luck and the goddess' blessing, the fields will be ready for ploughing soon. In the coastal villages the fisherfolk carefully check their boats for winter damage and begin to repair their nets.

Imbolg is about the first signs of spring, the promise of returning life, about sunlight and ripening and the growing conviction that the community will survive another year. Marion Green, who lives in England, brings the feeling to life as she says, "Mother Nature is seen as being renewed at this time; she becomes the Maiden of Spring, when the lambs' tails of hazel catkins tremble on the bare branches, and the hardiest of bulbs begin their new lease of life, thrusting green spears through the thawing mould. . . . The gamboling lambs seemed to herald the warmer days to come, and overhead, the harbingers of spring, the overwintering birds, were beginning to verbally stake their claims on their territory and sing a song of mating as the weeks of February passed by."[8]

After a long, hard winter, who could look forward to all this and not want to celebrate?

The Norse Festivals of February

In this season of abundant celebrations, the Norse were by no means lacking in the festival spirit. Prudence Priest, an Asatru priestess, explains that "Among Norse/ Teutonic heathens 'Valentine's Day' has long been celebrated as the Feast of Vali, the Honor of Vara, and even occasionally as the climax of Barri. These heathens are known for their rowdy celebrations. . . ."[9]

The Feast of Vali is a solar festival marking the strengthening power of the sun, the beginning of the end of winter, and the survival of the community. It also celebrates loyalty and kinship, and is named after Vali, a son of Woden whose role in mythology was to avenge the death of the beloved god Baldur.

The Honor of Vara is a lunar festival in which the community witnesses and celebrates the vows of lovers. Vara is the goddess who hears us when we swear oaths or make promises, and stands for truth and responsibility. She has been called "the Norse Athena," and is also analogous to Ma'at, the Egyptian goddess of truth. Vara is a companion of Freya, "The Lady," who is essentially the Norse Queen of the Gods.

Barri is a fertility festival that technically takes place at the lunar New Year, though most Norse religionists simply celebrate it beginning February 1 or 2 and until the full moon in Leo. It commemorates the courtship of the giantess Gerda, symbolizing Mother Earth, by Freyr, god of fertility and the power of the waxing sun.

The Norse also celebrated Imbolg under the name *Disting-tid*. This was the occasion for the "Charming of the Plow," when, as spring approached, plows would be dragged out of winter storage and blessed so that the harvests would be abundant. The event was also a celebration of the first breaking of the ground by metal, which was a huge technological leap from wooden plows. To our ancestors it meant that more land could be cultivated, and thus abundant food produced for their families; a village's chances of surviving the winter were enormously improved.

The festival's mythology includes the dwarves, who were both legendary miners of metal from the ground and masters of smithcraft, and crafted the magickal tools for the gods—everything from Thor's hammer to Frey's boat.[10] This element of Disting-tid echoes the stories of Brigit, who was the Celtic goddess of smiths. It is, then, doubly appropriate to bless the tools of any craftsperson or artisan on this day. Among Wiccans, ritual tools such as chalices, wands, and pentacles are often cleansed and consecrated at this time.

Festivals of the British Isles

The British Isles have seen many waves of invasion, and it would not have been surprising if the Anglos, Saxons, and Jutes of northern Europe had brought very different customs to Celtic England. Yet it seems their customs for this season were quite harmonious with Imbolg.

The second moon or "monath" of Anglo-Saxon England (circa 700 C.E.) was called *solmōnath* or "cake-month" by the Venerable Bede, a scholarly monk of the era. Jarman Lord, a modern Pagan linguist, believes that Bede misheard ". . . *suhlmōnath*, or 'Plow-month,' the month when the plow was charmed."[11] This would be an interesting parallel to modern Pagan practice, when ritual tools are consecrated at the first of February. Lord suggests that Suhlmōnath was also the occasion of *Ewemeoluc* . . . "the day the ewes come into milk." For Celt or Saxon, the facts of life were the same.

The festival that is called the Feast Day of Saint Brigid in Ireland is known as Laa'l Breeshey on the Isle of Man, halfway between Ireland and Wales. The Manx believe that Brigid came to the Isle of Man to receive the veil from Saint Maughold.

To commemorate the event, the lady of the house would gather green rushes, then stand on the threshold and invite Saint Brigid to enter and stay the night. In Manx, she would call out:

> *Brede, Brede, tar gys my thie tar dyn thie ayms noght*
> *Foshil jee yn dorrys da Brede, as ihig da Brede e heet staigh,*

Which translates as:

> *Brigid, Brigid, come to my house, come to my house tonight.*
> *Open the door for Brigid, and let Brigid come in.*

Then the rushes were placed by the hearth as a bed for the saint.[12]

Author Marion Green describes a festival held in St. Ives, Cornwall, at the beginning of February. People of all ages take part, and many enjoy guising, or dressing in fancy masks and costumes. Local musicians entertain the crowd as they gather to dress Saint Ea's well with early spring flowers and ivy. Saint Ea, it is said, arrived from Ireland floating on an ivy leaf. The well cures eye complaints and poor eyesight, and runs even in the driest summers.

In the churchyard "a silver ball is tossed against the church wall and when it falls among the gathered people it is carried off, usually by the younger villagers. As the church clock starts to strike twelve whoever has the ball is rewarded with a small money prize. Sometimes new pennies which have been heated up are thrown for the children to catch from the balcony of the town hall. Both the shiny silver ball and the bright, hot new pennies represent ancient symbols of the Sun whose power is being reawakened to bring about the warmer days of spring."[13]

Once again the immemorial themes of water and fire are at the heart of a February celebration. One wonders, though, just how hot those pennies were; and whether the healing powers of Saint Ea's well extended to toasted fingers.

February 1 is also the Wives' Feast in Ireland, and the Wives' Feast Day in northern England, once the Celtic kingdom of Brigantia. On this day women are honored as the preservers of the home and community. It is appropriately celebrated by making dinner for the lady of the house, and presenting small gifts to her and for the household. While no connection with the arrival of spring is immediately evident, the fire theme reappears: women are honored in part as keepers of the hearth.

Brigit's Eve, the Feast Day of Saint Brigid

If February 1 and 2 belong to anyone, they belong to Brigit—the Celtic goddess of Ireland who may be the same personage venerated by Catholics worldwide as Saint Brigid. (In our research, we found that the commonly accepted spelling of the name of the goddess is Brigit, and the commonly accepted spelling of the name of the saint is Brigid.)

Her festival is a time when "home and hearth were cleaned and blessed, a new fire was kindled, offerings of reparation were given, and peace was made. . . ."[14] Chapters 2 and 3 will be devoted to her mythology, her reported life as an abbess in fourth- and fifth-century Ireland, and the customs and traditions surrounding her legend. We will see all the strands and symbols of the season—lambs and light, fertility and warmth, hope and magic—come together in Brigit's story.

Candlemas

The early Roman Church frequently adopted the dates of Pagan festivals and invested them with Christian meanings, so as to encourage conversions to what was then a new religion. The theology might be different, but the timing of the seasonal celebrations was familiar. Christmas was placed near Yule, Easter near Ostara, Lammas at Lughnassad, and so on.

February 2 was not only the date of Celtic Imbolg, it was the day honoring Juno Februata as the virgin mother of Mars, the goddess who brought the fever (*febris*) of love to the world. (Christian authorities said the Pagan people went about Rome with "candles burning in worship of this woman Februa.") A festival so important to Pagans everywhere was a prime target for co-optation by the Church. Pope Sergius renamed the holy day in order to "undo this foul use and custome, and turn it onto God's worship and our Lady's . . . so that now this feast is solemnly hallowed throughout all Christendom."[15]

Thus February 2 was selected for the Feast of the Purification of the Virgin. This date was forty days after Christmas, the time span required in Jewish law for a woman to be considered cleansed after the birth of a son. (Had Jesus been a girl, eighty days would have been required, and the Festival of the Purification would have taken place about March 14.)[16] At any rate, this was the day that Mary took the baby Jesus to the Temple, where it was prophesied that he would be a Light to the World.

The other new name for this holy day was Candlemas. The name would appear to refer to a Catholic mass at which the candles were blessed. However, Jarman Lord, a researcher into Saxon religion, believes that "the suffix 'mas' probably does not refer to a Catholic mass. Quite the reverse. The Anglo-Saxons were likely to term any feast day a *maest*, meaning "food-mixture" or "feast"; the term was their own. And we may be very sure our ancestors feasted every chance they got."[17]

However the name arose, Christians embraced the wonderful symbolism of candlelight. In England, which could be very gray and gloomy during February, "the shadowy recesses of medieval churches twinkled brightly as each member of the congregation carried a lighted candle in procession around the church, to be blessed by the priest. Afterwards, the candles were brought home to be used to keep away storms, demons and other evils."[18] The custom was banned during the

Reformation because it smacked of Pagan magic. However, candlelight has proven far too popular as an adjunct of ritual to disappear quietly into the night; today, the descendants of those stern Protestant reformers enjoy candles on their altars.

The Feast Day of Saint Blaise

February 3 is the feast day of Saint Blaise, Blasius, or Blazey, an Armenian bishop who was martyred about 316 C.E. Blaise was a physician who became a Christian priest, and during the persecutions was denounced by the Roman governor Agricolaus. The governor's men tracked Blaise to a cave hidden in the forest, and found him surrounded by wild animals.[17] Despite this distraction, the soldiers managed to arrest and imprison him. While in prison he saved the life of a boy who was choking on a fishbone, and this was considered miraculous.

Blasius was quite popular during the Middle Ages, probably because he was thought to perform miraculous cures for both people with throat troubles, and animals. Priests performed a special blessing in his name: two candles were consecrated, held crossed together, and touched to the throat of the churchgoer, intoning the words "May God at the intercession of Saint Blasius preserve you from throat troubles and every other evil."[19]

Saint Blaise is not well documented; The *Catholic Encyclopedia* states candidly that "All the particulars concerning his life and martyrdom which are found in the Acts are purely legendary and have no claim to historical worth."[20]

He does appear in various Pagan mythologies, and even in the legends of King Arthur, where he was Merlin's teacher and mentor.[21] Other sources suggest that Blaise is actually Brigid in disguise. (How Brigid, either as a Celtic goddess or an Irish nun, could metamorphose into a male Armenian bishop is not entirely clear.) It is true that Blaise, like Brigid, is connected with fire; it may be that the word "blaze" comes directly from his name.[22]

There is yet another intriguing theory about his origins, explained by Barbara Walker. She believes that Blaise was a ". . . Spurious canonization of the Slavic horse-god Vlaise, or Vlas, or Volos: a consort of the lunar Diana. He was Christianized about the eighth century, but kept his pagan function as a patron of animals."[23]

Saint Valentine's Day

Valentine's Day is another of those Christian holidays that happened to land on a Pagan celebration and eventually replace it—sort of. It is based on the legend of Valentine, a priest who lived in Rome during the reign of Emperor Claudius II. According to legend, Claudius had a problem: nobody wanted to join the Roman army, and empires need big armies. Few men wanted to leave their families and march into a howling wilderness on the edge of nowhere to be slaughtered by barbarians—despite the handsome pay: a few ounces of salt each week. In the best tradition of psychotic emperors (remember the one who made his horse a Roman Senator?), Claudius decreed that all engagements and marriages would be banned henceforth. In theory, the men of Rome would instantly give up their girlfriends, look around for something equally enjoyable, and notice the recruiting posters. In practice, most of them continued to prefer the company of women to the lure of armed service, and many of them wound up getting secretly married.

Valentine was one of the priests who were willing to defy the emperor's ban and perform clandestine wedding ceremonies for the lovelorn. Imagine a hushed ceremony deep in the catacombs: lovers staring soulfully into each other's eyes, the mood suddenly broken by the harsh sound of marching Roman soldiers.

Valentine was arrested and sentenced to death. On the positive side, lots of well-wishers sent him flowers during his incarceration. The jailer's daughter, in particu-

lar, spent lots of time with him trying to cheer him up. Just before his execution, he sent her a nice thank-you note and signed it "Love from Your Valentine." He was executed on February 14, 269 C.E.; ironically, the holiday honoring Juno, goddess of women and marriage.

In 496, the Pope declared Valentine a saint and February 14 his feast day. During the Middle Ages the Lupercalia custom of drawing names from a bowl resurfaced, and celebrants would literally wear the names of their temporary boy- or girlfriend on their sleeves. A few centuries later, the custom of sending flowers became popular, and with expanded literacy, Valentine's Day cards became popular.

As Campanelli has pointed out, ". . . neither the most contemporary of Valentine's cards nor even antique ones of the most delicate paper lace show pictures of a martyred saint. Rather they show pictures of Cupid, son of Venus, Goddess of Love, identified by his bow and quiver of arrows."[24] It seems that the Pagan spirit of Lupercalia still survives in a new guise.

More Festivals of February

Everyone seems to want to celebrate in February. Here is a tiny sampling from around the world.

January 31 to February 3: THE FEAST OF ISIS, the Egyptian Mother Goddess, patroness of magick and healing. Although the seasons in Egypt are not the same as those of northern Europe, Isis is a good choice for any celebration of light and life.[25]

February 2: A Yoruba/Santeria feast day in honor of OYA, the Orisha of death and rebirth. Though Olodumare is worshipped as the one god, he has many Orishas, who are his aspects and messengers.[26] The transition from winter to spring can be seen as moving from death to rebirth.

February 4: This date marks SETSUBUN, the Japanese Bean Throwing and Lantern Festival. "Some ancient cultures believed that departed souls lived in beans. Think of the spirit of winter living in some dry beans and toss them away from you to symbolically send winter away. Light lanterns to encourage the return of light and warmth."[27]

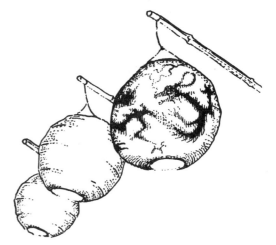

February 10: LI CHUM is the Chinese Spring Festival. It's a good time to arrange a vase of spring flowers and begin thinking about your garden.[28]

Varying Dates: As the great dragon turns the Wheel of the Year, the lunar-based CHINESE NEW YEAR[29] falls on different dates each time it comes around. The celebrations last fifteen days, and each day has a different theme. For example, on the second day dogs get extra food and attention, because that is believed to be the birthday of all dogs. On the fifth day, called Po Woo, people stay home to welcome the God of Wealth.

On New Year's Eve, ancestors who have passed on are honored at a banquet called *weilu*, which means "surrounding the stove." The stove is just as important to the Chinese as the hearth is to the Irish gathered around the fire to celebrate Brigid's arrival. Here Chinese families used to have a little shrine with a picture of the "kitchen god" in it.

There will be feasting: fish and chicken, noodles and meat dumplings, oranges and tangerines, sweet rice pudding, and a special candy tray. Each food has a symbolic meaning, such as prosperity, togetherness, or long life.

Many people wear red at this time because it is a bright and cheerful color, sure to bring good luck. The living rooms are decorated with live blooming plants and beautiful flowers to represent the return of spring and the reawakening of nature. Poetic couplets are written on red paper and placed on the doors; they have wishes such as: "May the Star of Happiness, the Star of Wealth, and the Star of Longevity shine on you."

On New Year's Eve, firecrackers are set off to welcome the New Year, and people dance the Lion Dance to vigorous drumming. At midnight, every door and window is opened to let the old year out.

What happens at the New Year sets the tone for the entire year. Therefore all debts are paid, bad language and unlucky words are avoided, and death and the past year are never mentioned. The whole focus is on a positive and happy future.

There are many parallels with the festivals of Europe. The Chinese New Year is a celebration of spring and new beginnings. There are feasts lit by candles and lanterns, and decorated with spring flowers. Houses are thoroughly cleaned, recalling the purification and cleansing themes of the Lupercalia. The hopes of peoples from different cultures a continent apart are often expressed in similar ways.

And surely we would all welcome the sentiment *Kung hay fat choi*— "Wishing you to prosper," the traditional Chinese New Year's greeting.

About February 28: The Chinese FEAST OF LANTERNS is an opportunity to encourage the return of light and warmth; hold a party with lots of colorful lanterns and put a light in the window overnight. "Lanterns are hung from high poles and carried in procession. . . . Some representing animals, birds, and very importantly the dragon. The high point of traditional celebration is the parade or dance of the dragon. The creature is made on a long framework of bamboo (up to or over 100 feet long!) and covered with bright paper or silk. . . . Temples, homes, and trees were strung with lanterns for dazzling light and beauty as soon as dusk came. Here is [part of] a poem written over five hundred years ago by Xin Qiji on such a festival occasion:

An easterly breeze prompts a thousand trees to bloom at night,
It also blows [the blossoms] off, which fall like a rain of stars. . . .
The flute is heard in the air,
The lights of the jade-like lanterns are glittering.
All night the lanterns of fish and dragons keep dancing. . . .[30]

Late February or early March: HOLI, the Festival of Colour, is a Hindu festival celebrating spring. Celebrants take buckets full of brightly colored water and drench one another, in imitation of the deities Krishna and Radha who splashed each other in the river on a fine spring day. Caste and gender barriers are forgotten, and everyone enjoys delicious foods. The night before, an image of Holika is burned on a big bonfire; Holika was the villainess in an ancient legend about a noble prince.[31]

Varying Dates: The more modern SAPPORO SNOW FESTIVAL brings thousands of snow sculptors and more than two million sightseers to the island of Hokkaido in Japan each February. Teams of sculptors create hundreds of giant statues from snow: gods, mythological figures, cartoon heroes, dinosaurs, and even great castles. A single sculpture may require several hundred truckloads of snow.

The chances are that Brigit would delight in the inspirational and artistic energy of Sapporo. The sculptures themselves disappear after a few days; like the snows from which they are formed, and the winter itself, they are just one part of the cycle—and must make way for spring.

The Themes of the Holy Day

We are so diverse, we humans, and yet so much alike in the deep recesses of our spirits. If we could bring together, in some winter village outside of time and space, a sampling of our species, what might happen? Imagine an Irish girl of the seventeenth century, a Mongol soldier from the Khan's army, a priest of Faunus from classical Rome, an aristocratic Egyptian lady who prayed to Isis, and a Saxon farmer from the Dark Ages. As the winter darkness gave way to light and warmth, and the first spring flowers pushed through the snow, would they not find a way celebrate together? After one year or several, would there not be a feast by candle-light, and homage to the sun, and windows open to the fresh air for spring clean-ing? Wherever people gather and find any reason for hope, there is celebration.

These are the common themes that run through the complex of midwinter holy days: First, there is the theme of returning light, the first signs of spring, and the promise of renewed life and fertility. This is usually associated with the sun, and sometimes with fire generally. Second, we find the theme of practices of outer and inner cleansing—everything from house-cleaning to washing one's body to spiri-tual purification. And third, there is the theme of initiation; echoing the new beginnings associated with spring, the idea that individual human beings can "die" to their old lives and be spiritually "reborn" into a higher spiritual state. These themes will be explored more deeply in the chapters ahead; let us continue the journey with a visit to a goddess.

Notes

1. *Gimbutas, Gods and Goddesses of Old Europe*, pp. 190–195.

2. Ibid.

3. McCoy, *The Sabbats*, p. 98.

4. Farrar, *Eight Sabbats*, p. 65.

5. Manning-Sanders, *Festivals*, pp. 43–44.

6. Campanelli, *Ancient Ways*, p. 2.

7. Farrar, pp. 61–62.

8. Green, *A Calendar of Festivals*, p. 18.

9. Letter from Prudence Priest to *The COG Newsletter,* author's files.

10. ADF Neopagan Druidism website.

11. Jarman Lord, "The Anglo-Saxon Year Division," files of Amber K; original publication source unknown.

12. From the files of Amber K, source unknown.

13. Green, p. 19.

14. *Crescent 2000*, RCG

15. Walker, *A Woman's Encyclopedia*, pp. 134–135.

16. Leviticus 12:2–5.

17. Lord.

18. Chalice Center online.

19. "Saint Blaise," *Catholic Encyclopedia* online.

20. Ibid.

21. Green, p. 21.

22. McCoy, pp. 87–88.

23. Walker, p. 110.

24. Campanelli, *Ancient Ways*, p. 25.

25. *Crescent 2000*, RCG.

26. Ibid.

27. *Festivals Together,* pp. 40–41.

28. *Crescent 2000*, RCG.

29. The following sources were used for this section:
    Marco Polo, quoted in Manning-Sanders, *Festivals*, pp. 42–43.
    Fitzjohn et al, *Festivals Together,* pp. 202–213.
    San Diego's Chinese Community Home Page.
    China website.

30. *Festivals Together,* p. 38.

31. Ibid. pp. 40–41.

Brigit, Goddess and Saint

February 1 is the feast day of Brigit, that mysterious figure who was a primary goddess of the Celtic peoples, yet whose legends were not written down until centuries after the time of the Christian Saint Brigid—an Irish abbess who may have lived (if she existed at all) in the fifth and sixth centuries C.E.

For someone who may have been a myth, Brigit is revealed in biography, myth, and legend as an extraordinarily powerful, loving, and vital person. She is a bundle of contradictions that add up to a singular whole, a personage of fire and water, of will and compassion, intensely focused on her mission of protection and care for her people. She is a healer who is also a warrior, a humble milkmaid who commands miracles from God, a goddess of fertility best known to Catholics as a holy virgin.

A modern website describes her appeal well:

> Brighid is such a powerful archetype for these times because she
> speaks to diverse groups of people and crosses all barriers. To
> those who follow pre-Christian spirituality in one form or anoth-
> er, she is accepted as the Triple Goddess, Patroness of Poetry,
> Healing and Smithcraft, Lady of the Sacred Flame and the Heal-
> ing Waters. To those who follow Christian traditions, she is St.
> Brighid, a very real woman who lived during not so distant histo-
> ry. To poets and artists of all kinds, she is the Muse. The descrip-
> tion of her in each tradition is exactly the same![1]

We shall examine her legend first as goddess, then we will look at the story of
the saint, and then explore the connections between them.

We do not know whether Brigit began as a natural force like fire, later humanized,
or as a human being, later deified. We do know that she is a lady of great antiqui-
ty, who has been with us—if not for hundreds of thousands of years, at least for a
couple of millennia. She is one of the great goddesses, who can be ranked with
Isis and Ishtar and Hera and Freya. She has her own face, a vast sphere of inter-
ests, mighty powers, and perhaps even a few stories.

Her legends were handed down through the generations in an oral tradition
that was eroded and then largely assimilated into the new faith of Christianity.
With the loss of the Druidic bards, their vast knowledge was lost as well.

Hardly any of Brigit's mythology has been recorded, despite the fact that she
was. ". . . a deity so high that her brass shoe was the most sacred object that could
be imagined, a divinity so intensely related to the feminine force that no man was
allowed to pass beyond the hedge surrounding her sanctuary."[2]

We can guess that many of the tales told of Saint Brigid were actually myths
about the goddess, who was either confused with the Irish saint or co-opted by
the Church in order to seduce the Pagan populace to the new religion. But written
references to Brigit as goddess do not appear until hundreds of years after the
saint's life was chronicled.[3]

Brigit is often depicted as a triple goddess. When she is shown as a solitary figure, most often as Brigantia in Romano-British statuary, she carries a spear and an orb or globe, the symbol of sovereignty. In some references she wears a green mantle, which may be a sign of her connection to the Faery Folk. A few references hint that she was blonde and slender. Older, Celtic stone images that may depict her are crude and not at all flattering. Unless we are to believe that the Celts pictured her as bald with sunken eyes and a big nose, they tell us little beyond the fact that she is probably a very ancient deity.

The Goddess by Many Names

The Celtic goddess was known both on the mainland of Europe and in the British Isles under many easily recognizable variants of her name. Some of her many names, or possibly titles, include:

Breo-Saighit, Brede, Bride (Scottish), Brigit (Irish), Bridget (Swedish), Brigandu (French), Brigantia (N. English), and Ffraid (pronounced "frrȳ-ed") (Welsh).

The most ancient form of her name, at least in Ireland, was Brigit; but later it became Brigid, with a hard "g." In modern Gaelic it is usually spelled Brighid, and pronounced "Bree-id."[4]

Since Brigit is the Old Irish form of her name, we will use Brigit throughout this book when referring to the goddess, and Brigid for the saint. (It is simplest to pronounce both as "Bree-id.") Both versions derive from the Old Celtic *briganti* which in turn derives from Indo-European *bhrghnti*. The Sanskrit cognate *bhrati* or *brihati* means 'the exalted one,' and may have originally been more a title than a proper name.

In folklore, Brigit means "fiery arrow," "bright arrow," or "the bright one." According to modern etymology, none of these are accurate, but they are certainly descriptive of her personality. Kondratiev agrees: "In many ways 'fiery arrow' is a fitting name for Brigit since in one image it conveys the idea of the bright flame that has come to be associated with her, along with a sense of her directness, her ability to get straight to the point and the force of her energy. . . . The rays of the sun may also be described as fiery arrows."[5]

The Origin of the Goddess

Barbara Walker tells us that Brigit immigrated to Ireland "with the Gaelic Celts from their original home in Galatia. One of her earliest shrines was Brigeto in Illyricum."[6] In Austria a tribe called the Brigantii lived near Bregenz. The Sanskrit roots of her name hint that she may have migrated west from ancient India; but if so, what was her original name, and was she an ancestress of Hindu goddesses known today, such as Sarasvati?

No one can be sure just how ancient Brigid is, or where her original roots lie. Celtic oral traditions probably included stories and poems about Brigit, as well as more information on her lineage. But oral traditions are fragile; they last only as long as the culture is intact and the bards or story-tellers pass on the information to apprentices. War with Rome made that difficult.

Wherever she came from, she certainly flourished in Ireland and Britain. Today hundreds of places in Ireland bear her name, such as Brideswell and Remplebride, and many parishes called Kilbride. She was the special goddess of Leinster, and in many stories Saint Brigit deals with the king of that region. Even London has its Bridewell, or Brigit-well.

As Brigantia or "High One," she gave her name to the Celtic lands which included the north of England and parts of Spain and France. The Brigantes named rivers for her, and Yorkshire was particularly fervent in her worship. Her name is seen in Breconshire, Wales, and in Brechin, Scotland.

Not only her names, but her more formal titles were legion. Some of these, from both ancient sources and modern, include the following[7]: Brigit the Victorious; Brighid of the Immortal Host; Brighid of the Slim Fairy Folk; Bride of Joy; Mother of Songs and Music; The Lady of the Sea; Mountain-traveler; The Flame in the Heart of All Women[8]; Ashless Flame[9]; Flame of Two Eternities[10]; Mother of All Wisdom[11]; and Heavenly Brigantia.[12] Of course these are merely the English translations. In Gaelic they can be a little daunting; for example, Song-sweet Brighid of the Tribe of the Green Mantles is *Brighid-Binne-Bheule-Ihuchd-nan-trusganan-uaine.*

A proverb says that "a child who is loved has many names." If the same folk wisdom applies to deities, then this goddess must have been beloved indeed, by many, many people over a very long time. And even deities have families who love them; let us look at Brigit's relations.

Family Relationships

Brigit is one of the Tuatha de Danaan, or people of the goddess Danu. Her mother may have been the goddess Boann, for whom the River Boyne is named. This in turn appears to come from *bo/-fhionn* (white cow, she of white cattle), a name cognate with the Sanskrit Govinda.[13]

In some legends Brigit is described as the daughter of the Dagda, the Celtic "Father of All" and "Lord of Great Knowledge," a warrior and protector, who was paired with the Morrigan. Other sources say that Brigit was his consort, not his daughter. Dagda is a god of abundance, who fed the world with his cauldron called Undry. He carried a huge club that required nine ordinary men to lift, and while he could slay with the one end, with the other he could bring the dead back to life. This seems to reflect the Celts' understanding that death and rebirth were part of the same cycle of existence, and echoes Brigit's attributes: goddess of fertility and birth, yet also a warrior.

In her aspect of Brigh, she loved Bres the Beautiful, the ruler of the Children of Danu. Bres was sometimes described as half Fomorian, the race which ruled Ireland before the Tuatha de Danaan arrived. "In the myth of the battle of Magh Tuiredh, which chronicles the great conflict between the Tuatha De Danaan and their demon-enemies the Fomorians for the possession of Ireland, Brigit appeared as mediator between the two. . . . Here Brigit is presented as an ancestor-deity, a mother-goddess whose main concern was the future well-being of Ireland."[14] Bres and Brigh had a son Ruadan, who was later killed when he took arms against Goibniu, the smith god of Ireland. All in all, the myths hint that Brigit was a bridge between the warring peoples, and her son Ruadan—part Danaan, part Fomorian—may have been a symbol of their eventual merging. It is perhaps an ominous portent of Ireland's later troubles that Ruadan was killed by the gods.

There are hints that Brigit may have had an older persona as the Lady of the Sea, daughter of Lir, the god of the oceans. The legend is described beautifully in Fiona MacLeod's novel *Winged Destiny*, where Brigit "had lost her brother Manan the Beautiful, but . . . brought him back again, so that the world of men rejoiced, and ships sailed the sea in safety and nets were filled with the fruit of the wave."[15] It is very possible that the Brigit we know, or know a little about, was a merging of two distinct goddesses, much as Pallas and Athena. Perhaps the deity who arrived from the east with the Children of Danu blended with an ancestral sea goddess of the Fomorians.

This is a sparse family tree for such an important deity. Brigid the saint had a more detailed genealogy. Probably most of the goddess' lineage was lost with the traditions of the Celts. Or perhaps if the saint's lineage were to be examined more closely, her ancestors might turn out to be Celtic gods rather than human chieftains.

Brigit's Connections with Other Goddesses

The Brigantes, possibly attempting to explain her to the Romans, identified Brigit with Juno, the Queen of Heaven. She has also been compared with the Roman goddesses Minerva, patron of wisdom and handicrafts; Vesta, a virgin fire goddess; and Victory. Brigit also has some traits in common with the ancient Greek goddess Hecate,[16] including her status as a goddess of liminality, one who stands at the boundary of different worlds. Any crossroads where three paths met was sacred to Hecate; but for Brigit, the place was sacred where three *streams* came together, and sacrifices of milk and flowers were left for her there.[17] As a goddess of the hearth-fire, Brigit also has much in common with the Greek Hestia. Miranda Green believes that she is also similar in important ways to Greek Artemis and Roman Diana: "She remained a virgin but one of her most prominent roles was as a provider of plenty, like a mother-goddess, and she was also a patron of pregnant women. . . . Although virgin, she stimulated fertility. . . ."[18]

She is further linked with Tanit, the Dea Celestis (Heavenly Goddess) from which she gets her title "Caelestis Brigantia." Some say that she is related to Lucifer via a saint, Santa Lucia. Lucia is represented as a maid with a crown of candles, and her name "is obviously a feminine form of the name Lucifer, the Light Bearer, who in Italian traditions is the brother/consort of Diana, Maiden Goddess of the Moon. To the ancient Greeks, [Lucifer] is the son of the Goddess Eos, Goddess of the sunrise and is identified with the morning star."[19]

Brigit is not only a goddess of fire, but also a deity famous for her healing springs and wells—a water goddess. Some believe that the Celtic Sulis, the goddess of springs, is another face of Brigit. Sulis was adopted by the Romans and honored at Aquea Sulis. Her name means "eye" but also "sun."[20] So we have a fire or sun goddess, Brigit, whose sacred places are mostly springs and wells; and a goddess of springs, Sulis, who is called "Sun."

In some cases, one goddess may have evolved from another in the dim prehistoric past. But even when their origins were completely distinct, different tribes and nations looked for common characteristics in their deities to better understand and relate one to another: "You have a fire-goddess? What's yours called? Ours is Brigit; maybe they are the same goddess, and we just use different names."

Mythology is filled with tales of goddesses who have double or even triple aspects, such as the joyful Egyptian Bast whose other face is the violent Sekhmet. Brigit is another in this tradition, "typical of the universal Goddess of Fertility. Her counterpart in Celtic traditions is the Cailliach, or Crone. In some traditions the Maiden is [also] the Cailliach, beautiful on one side, dark and ugly on the other, bringing life and fertility on one hand, death and destruction on the other."[21] Lady Gregory, a collector of Irish folklore, confirms that "Brigit . . . had two faces, one that is young and

comely and one that is old and terrible . . . some people assert that [Brigit and the Cailleach] are two sides of the same being."[22]

A wonderful Scottish tale tells of the goddess who is both Crone and Maiden: "On the eve of [Saint Brigid's Day], the Old Woman of Winter, the Cailleach, journeys to the magical isle in whose woods lies the miraculous Well of Youth. At the first glimmer of dawn, she drinks the water that bubbles in a crevice of a rock, and is transformed into Bride, the fair maid whose white wand turns the bare earth green again."[23]

The two are not always so closely identified in the old myths. Patricia Monaghan relates a pre-Celtic story in which:

> . . . the Cailleach kept a maiden named Bride imprisoned in the high mountains of Ben Nevis. But her own son fell in love with the girl and, at winter's end, he eloped with her. The hag chased them across the landscape, causing fierce storms as she went, but finally she turned to stone as Bride was freed. In such stories, which may date back as far as 2,000 to 3,000 years, Brigid becomes a surrogate for a spring/summer goddess whose rule over the land alternated with that of a fall/winter hag."[24]

Campanelli compares the Bride/Calleach pairing to Greco-Roman deities: Demeter and Persephone, as well as Ceres and Proserpina. Like the Cailleach who is the spirit of Winter and becomes enraged when her child elopes, Demeter's anger leaves the earth cold and lifeless when her daughter is taken away. Just as Demeter is both bountiful Mother and Winter Hag, her daughter Persephone is the Spring Maiden and also the Queen of the Underworld, land of death. This resonance between mother and daughter, life and death, spring and winter, and goddesses who each embody both aspects, is very ancient in European mythologies.[25]

Where the Goddess Rules

Every deity has realms that he or she rules, whether it be the sea, the underworld, or all creation. Brigit is first of all a goddess of sovereignty. She may have been a western equivalent of Epona, the white mare-goddess, whom kings had to symbolically marry in order to govern in her name. "She was the most popular form of the sovereignty goddess throughout the Celtic world. The Welsh word for king, 'brenin,' is thought to mean 'consort of Brigantia.'"[26] "*Bruide*, the Pictish royal throne name, is said to derive from the Pagan Goddess Brigid. The Bruide name was given to each Pagan Pictish king who was viewed as the male manifestation of the spirit of the Goddess."[27] In her aspect as Brigantia, she has been depicted crowned, holding a globe and spear.

Brigit the Fire Goddess

Brigit is a fire deity and perhaps a sun goddess. In a biography of Saint Brigid from *The Book of Lismore*, a Druid prophesies that she will be "a daughter conspicuous and radiant, who will shine like the sun among the stars of heaven"—a very goddess-like description. Many gods and goddesses were connected with light or fire; words such as deity and divinity are related to the Indo-European words *div* or *dyu*, which mean "to shine." Brigit was no exception. She was especially linked to the growing light of late winter and the promise of spring's return: "The light of consciousness as her flame, Brighid guides us through the darkness, breathing new life into the land, bringing us into spring."[28]

Brigit, Fertility and Birth Goddess

Brigit's connection with the growing season brings us naturally enough into her role as a fertility goddess. She was the patroness of domestic animals and crops, and by extension the goddess of prosperity, since wealth in ancient Ireland meant large herds and bountiful harvests. Human fertility was also one of her concerns, since she was called upon to protect women in childbirth, and was said to be present, leaning over each cradle to guard the newborn child. A very old tradition involves making a "Bride's Bed" on the evening of her festival, where a phallic wand is placed in the "bed" with a doll representing the goddess; a fertility charm if ever there was one (see chapter 3). Although scholars say the words have different roots, it is interesting that one of Brigit's names, "Bride," is also the term for a young (and usually fertile) woman getting married.

She is also patroness of midwifery: ". . . in the Hebrides she would be ritually asked, by one of the women in attendance, to come into the house when a woman was giving birth . . . in some sense Bride can be seen as the midwife at the birth of the coming spring."[29]

Today she is best known as a triple goddess of poetry, healing, and smithcraft. It is Brigit who guides "the fire of the poet's heart, of the healer's hands and the fire used by the smith."[30] Author Lisa Spindler explains it this way: "Brighid's three aspects are (1) Fire of Inspiration as patroness of poetry, (2) Fire of the Hearth, as patroness of healing and fertility, and (3) Fire of the Forge, as patroness of smithcraft and martial arts."[31] Let's look at each of these roles.

Brigit the Healer

As Healer, Brigit taught leechcraft and the properties of healing herbs, and was patroness of dozens of sacred springs and wells that were said to have healing properties. These were sources of purification for both body and spirit. One legend tells "how a crystal drop from the mantle of Brigid touched the earth and became a deep and clear lake. This was said to be a lake from Tir-Na-Moe 'Land of the Living Heart' and there was healing in it for all weariness and battle wounds."[32]

Many of these wells are still destinations for pilgrimages today, by modern Catholics venerating the saint and by others who seek her healing waters. Both sunlight and water were considered to be especially effective in curing ailments of the eyes, which was one of the goddess' specialties. In addition her mantle, and any fabric blessed by her, were said to be healing artifacts. She was the very first in Ireland to master the art of weaving, and into the cloth she placed healing threads that still exercised their benign powers centuries later.[33]

Brigit the Smith

As Smith, Brigit stands in company with other smith-gods such as Wayland of Britain, Hephaestus of Greece, and Vulcan of Rome. She ruled the mysteries of metalworking, an ancient art that aroused awe among early societies. To many people, smithcraft was pure magic: the smith could use fire to transform stone (the ore-bearing rock) into metal, then shape the metal into tools and weapons. This implied mastery over fire and matter both, and the secrets of the trade were treated more as religious mysteries than technical skills. Guilds taught their techniques only to initiates, and, to some, ". . . ores and metals were regarded as living organisms: one spoke in terms of their gestation, growth, birth, and even marriage. . . ."[34]

Brigit the Poet

As Source of Inspiration, Brigit held sway over poetry and other creative arts. In *Cormac's Glossary* she is spoken of as "Brigit the female sage . . . Brigit the goddess, whom poets adored, because her protecting care over them was very great and very famous." As the patroness of *filidhact*, poetry or bardic lore, she was essentially the nine Greek Muses enfolded into one Celtic deity. The bards who invoked her were far more than entertainers or wandering minstrels. In a largely non-literate society, they preserved spiritual wisdom, history, family and clan lineages, and mythology in songs and stories. They were the guardians of the soul of a people. Beyond that, they were powerful influences on the beliefs and opinions of the day; satire from the lips of a skilled bard was considered a deadly weapon.

> The high status of poets within Celtic societies is well attested and was maintained down to the seventeenth or eighteenth centuries. In Gaelic societies the name for a poet, *file* (or *filid,* plural), is derived from a root word meaning "to see." Celtic poets may be better known as bards. . . . Poets were expected to develop a knowledge of a huge number of traditional stories, of poetry and

legal matters as well as the skills to create his or her own poetry. Yet the basic inspiration could be gifted from otherworld sources.[36]

Poetry, or *filidhect*, was closely connected with seership, and therefore Brigid was seen as the inspirational force behind divination, the patroness of oracles.[37] The *Lebor Gabála Erenn* describes Brigid as "The Poetess" or banfil.[38]

Inspiration and poetry were closely linked with water in Brigit's domain. "Spring water symbolically unites the underworld and the upper world by rising out of the darkness of the earth and reflecting the light of the heavens. . . ."[39] In other words, the ideas and insights, the "understanding" that is hidden in the subconscious mind becomes revealed to the conscious, rational self. It is no wonder that holy wells and sacred springs are powerful sources of inspiration in Irish lore.

Brigit the Warrior

In her aspect as Brigantia, Brigit was a warrior and a teacher of the martial arts, a *briga*. Her soldiers were called brigands; the term was later transmuted by Christian society to mean thieves or highwaymen. It was not unknown for Celtic women to distinguish themselves as soldiers or war leaders, perhaps in part because they had Brigantia, Macha, Nemain, Babd Catha, and the Morrigan as inspiration and role models. They also heard stories of Scáthach, "the Shadowy One," a legendary warrior woman who trained Cuchulainn and other Irish heroes on the Island of Skye; and of course the very real, very human Boudicca, the Queen of the Iceni who twice led her warriors to vicory over the Roman legions in battle.

However, despite her military prowess, Brigit is by no means portrayed as bloodthirsty; she is also a mediator between warring factions, and a mother who mourns her son's death in war. When her beloved Ruadan was killed, Brigit created keening, "the *caoine* or lament, the mournful song of the bereaved Irishwoman."[40]

The Great Goddess

In conjunction with Brigit's role in fertility and childbirth, her association with war marks Brigit as one of the Great Goddesses of Life and Death; it puts her firmly on the same plane as Freya, Isis, and Diana. Yet she had a myriad of less exalted roles that were nonetheless important to farmers and housewives. She was goddess of agriculture and the household arts. Among these were weaving, dyeing, and making beer: "in many Celtic traditions, it's customary to pour out the first drink of home brew in honor of Brigit, who also takes on the duties of patron Goddess of Brewing."[41] She was able to turn her bath water into beer! Brigit is even mentioned as the goddess who invented whistling as a way to signal her friends in the darkness.

Her Nature as Triple Goddess

Was Brigit one goddess with various talents . . . or one goddess with three distinct aspects or personas . . . or three sister goddesses? One source says that "She is Ruler, Bringer of Prosperity; her two sisters display the alchemical sword and tongs of blacksmithing and the twin serpents connoting medical skill."[42]

A tenth-century source, *Cormac's Glossary (Sanas Cormaic),* hints that Brigit is the name of three separate goddesses. According to Walker, the triune deities were called "Three Blessed Ladies of Britain" or the "Three Mothers," and were identified with the moon[43] —though apparently not as Maiden, Mother, and Crone, the common arrangement of triple lunar goddesses elsewhere.

Brigit's Faery Connections

Irish mythology is ancient, complex, and many-layered. Eire has successively been inhabited by several races and cultures, and each added their own gods and legends to the rich mix.

According to L. MacDonald in his article "Celtic Folklore: The People of the Mounds," the Celts believed that ancestors, gods, and ancient peoples are all part of "an invisible realm inhabited by Otherworldly beings known collectively as the

Sidhe ["shee"], or the Good People. . . . The Sidhe are considered to be a distinct race, quite separate from human beings yet who have had much contact with mortals over the centuries. . . ."[44] The realm of the Sidhe is also called Faery.

The Sidhe come in many forms. Some walk on the earth, usually by twilight or after dark, who may be the descendants of the old cthonic Earth gods, and they live under the earth in hollow hills or fairy mounds. The "Sluagh Sidhe" fly through the air. The Sidhe are shape-shifters, giants, and of course the quintessentially Irish leprechauns, little people who may be "a folk memory of a dwarfish race of Fir Bolg people who lived in these raths before the coming of the Gaels."[45] Some of the Sidhe are essentially *genius loci*, the guardians of certain places in the natural landscape; of lakes and forests and mountains.

By no means are most of the Sidhe eerie or non-human in appearance. Often they are tall, slender, elegant, and well-spoken; so much so that the common term for them is "the gentry." They have their own kingdoms and aristocracy, and many of the great kings and queens of the Sidhe live on in legend.

MacDonald tells us that:

> "There are many great fairy queens that are remembered. . . . They are known as '*bean righean na brugh*', the fairy queen of the palace, and are quite clearly the tutelary goddesses of local tribes. Many are still said to be the guardians of certain Irish clans. . . . They include Aine, originally of Munster, ancestress of the O'Corry family. . . . Aoibheal of County Clare, an early queen of the O'Briens . . . [and] Cliodna of County Cork, guardian of the O'Keefes. . . ."[46]

The Tuatha de Danaan, who held the land when the Gaelic peoples arrived, are described as being highly intelligent, immortal, and almost godlike in their knowledge.

How does all this apply to Brigit? It is said that the goddess was of the Tuatha de Danaan branch of the Sidhe. Many clues confirm the fairy connection. Brigit is described as wearing a green cloak, and she is goddess of rulership; in *The Colloquoy of the Ancients*, Saint Patrick sees a fairy woman emerging from a cave "wearing a green mantle with a crown of gold on her head." (Scotland also has a form of banshee called "the Green Lady.")

Alexander Carmichael speaks of "*bean chaol a chot uaine 's na gruaige buidhe*', the slender woman of the green kirtle and yellow hair, who can turn water into wine."[47] Not only did Brigit have a magick kirtle or girdle, she was known for her golden hair, and one of her titles was "Brigit of the Slim Fairy Folk." And of course she could turn water to beer.

The Irish leave offerings of milk and butter on the porch to placate the Tuatha de Danaan for their defeat long ago. In Scotland "The *gruagach* is the fairy woman who watches over the cattle fold at night and protects the goodness of the milk. On Skye, Tiree, and other islands are to be found '*gruagach* stones', stones with hollows in which libations of milk were poured as an offering to her."[48]

In both lands, people leave milk and butter out as a gift to Brigit on her special day, February 1, because she is the patron of cattle and many of her stories are related to milk.

Recall that Brigit invented the *caoine,* the custom of keening a lament for the dead. MacDonald reminds us that "The most well known of the fairy women both in Ireland and Scotland has to be the *Bean Sidhe*, the Banshee. In Ireland she is the ancestress of the old aristocratic families, the Irish clans. When any death or misfortune is about to occur in the family, she will be heard wailing her unearthly lament. . . . She is also known as the *bean chaointe*, the wailing woman."[49]

Brigit was a goddess, yes; but she was also a Queen of Faery.

Brigit in Arthurian Legend

The Celtic Otherworld, Tir nan Og, was sometimes called the "Land of Women" or the "Land of Youth." Here there was a sacred grove of apple trees that later became known as Avalon in Arthurian legend. Brigit owned it; she was not the only goddess to have an orchard, since the Greek Hera and Norse Idun, or in some stories Freya, had similar magick apple trees.

Further, she may have been the smith who forged Excalibur, the Lady of the Lake who gave it to Arthur and later received it back, and the healer who took the "Once and Future King" away to Avalon as he lay dying.

Late additions to the story of Brigit? Perhaps. But among all the gods, who could better fulfill these roles?

Conclusion

Few gods or goddesses have the kind of breadth that Brigit exhibits, or the powers that she commands. As sparse as the records are, they hint at a deity who spans all things: fertility and birth; poetry and inspiration; the fires of the hearth, the forge, and the sun itself; the waters of springs, wells, and the very seas; the arts of rulership and the skills of war. She is Midwife and Lifegiver, Poet, Smith, Healer, Warrior, and Sovereign.

Where did this whole panopoly of legend, myth, and ancient religion begin? Was Brigit the culmination of eons of religious evolution, an attempt by ancient peoples to put a human face to the terrible mysteries of life and death? Or were the deities of the Celts based on tribal memories of great ancestors, those who led the great migrations and defended their clans in a new land?

In either case, it seems that later the gods and goddesses were displaced and became the Sidhe, in a misty realm of folk memory where deities live on after they have been supplanted by newer religions. Nothing is ever lost. Brigit lives, if she was a clan ancestress, in the genes of her descendants. She lives as a beloved aspect of the goddess in the hearts and rituals of modern Pagans. And she lives on, perhaps, as a saint of the Roman Catholic Church.

Brigid the Saint

What was life like, in Brigid's Ireland?

Old Ireland was divided into a patchwork of about 150 tiny kingdoms. Each local ruler gave homage to a more powerful monarch, who was in turn subject to one of the five provincial kings. Not until about 200 C.E. was the High Kingship established at Tara in County Meath, and even then there was little real centralized power.

Christianity first gained a foothold on the island around 350 C.E., though not in a form approved by Rome; the first monks were entirely too willing to blend their beliefs with the older Pagan practices. When the future Saint Brigid was reputedly born in the middle of the fifth Century, Ireland had entertained Christian missionaries for only about a hundred years.[50] King McNeill reigned, a son of the famous High King Niall of the Nine Hostages. The old Celtic gods were still honored by many, and the Druids very active, a "highly organized body of learned men with specialists in customary law, sacred arts, heroic literature, and genealogy."[51]

Ireland was a blend of many peoples, but unusual in Europe because it was never conquered by the Roman Empire. When the Romans took Bri-tain, beginning in 44 C.E., many people fled west to Ireland. They brought their knowledge, skills, and culture with them: England's loss was Ireland's gain.[52] In Brigid's time, about 476 C.E., the Romans abandoned their British province after centuries of peace and stability.

The land was green, the population sparse. Small villages existed, especially along the coast, but no real towns or great cities; three hundred years later, Dublin was still a smallish town of timber and wickerwork plastered with clay.[53] Most people lived in scattered farmsteads surrounded by low, round, defensive earthworks meant to discourage cattle raids. A few may have still lived in the ancient way in *crannógs*, small artificial islands in the lakes or bogs, designed for defense.

Although there was some farming in Ireland, the important families measured their wealth in cows, sheep, pigs, and domestic fowl. So-called "ring-money" of bronze, silver, and gold was used, but none of this was made in standard sizes or weights.

Society was stratified. The basic unit was the *fine* or extended family, followed by the *tuath* (tribe, clan, or small kingdom). Slavery was common, merchants were rare. A few artisans and craftsmen provided specialty items, but most people were farmers, herders, or fisherman. They answered to chiefs or landed gentry, and these in turn to the nobility.

Women could and did hold high office, from queens, to Druidesses, to warriors who sometimes taught the young male soldiers their craft. Most of these women were born to high rank, so in that respect early Ireland was like many societies, in which noblewomen have power and authority undreamed of by female commoners.

The people celebrated the old festivals of Imbolg and Samhain—pastoral festivals marking their heritage as herders rather than as farmers. In Brigid's era agriculture was improving; iron ploughshares that could turn a deep furrow were replacing the old wooden plows that barely scratched the soil.[54]

Ireland was a land prosperous enough, and mostly at peace. The ever-present cattle raids, the jockeying for power among the chiefs and kings, and occasional forays across the sea to Scotland for slaves and plunder kept things lively. The invasions of the Norse and the troubles with the English were far in the future, and life seemed good. This was Brigid's Ireland.

The Annals of Saint Brigid

Several biographies have been written of Saint Brigid, but none by anyone who knew her personally or even lived at the same time. Among her biographers were Saint Broccan Cloen, said to have died in 650, 125 years or more after Saint Brigid's death; Cogitosus, a monk of Kildare; Coelan, another Irish monk of about the same period; and Saints Ultan and Aileran.

Some authors believe that Saint Brigid is really a composite of several women from Ireland and Wales. In any case, the Celtic saint was popular in the Isle of Man, Wales, Cornwall, Scotland, and Brittany, as well as Ireland. In these varied places her titles as saint include Saint Bride of the Mantle, Saint Bride of the Isles (Scotland), and Golden-haired Bride of the Kine.

Much that is in the "lives" of Brigid sounds more like mythology or legends than the story of a human woman. So fabulous are her stories, and so sparse the evidence of her existence, that some say Saint Brigid was never an historical personage at all. Be that as it may, here is her story as explained by the early Irish monks.

Her Life and Times

Brigid may have been born between 439[55] and 452 C.E., and died between 518 and 525. Saint Patrick, who was an important part of her life, is supposed to have been born in 387, come to Ireland about 403 and, according to one source, died in 493, which would have made Brigid in her forties when he passed on[56]—and Patrick 106 years of age at his death! But other sources place his death much earlier.

Brigid was the daughter of a chieftain of the family of Etech in Leinster, whose name is sometimes given as Dubthach—"the Dark One," pronounced "Duffac." As the story goes, he fell in love with a slave at his court, a "handmayd" named Brocca or Broicsech (pronounced "Brocksheh," meaning a baby badger), and got her with child. In *The Book of Lismore* a wizard prophesied that Brocca would bear a daughter "conspicuous, radiant, who will shine like a sun among the stars of heaven." Dubthach's wife, "taking the matter very greefully,"—and who would not?—demanded that he get rid of Brocca; so he sold her to a magician, wizard, or Druid. This mysterious personage took her to the island of Iona, then known as "the Druid's Isle;" or to the village of Faughart near Dundalk, Louth, in Ireland; or possibly Uinmeras near Kildare, or Offaly in the Midlands, or somewhere in Connacht.[57] Obviously no one was much interested in documenting the travels of a slave.

At dawn one day, as she stepped across the threshold of her home, Brocca gave birth to Brigid. At that moment, a pillar of fire shot from Brigid's head to the heavens. Neighbors saw the fire and hastened to extinguish it, but found only a peaceful mother and baby.

Brigid's lineage was very important to the Irish. Her "princely ancestors" are emphasized, and simply repeating her genealogy was considered a powerful spell of protective magick. In the words of an old prayer:

> *The genealogy of the holy maiden Bride,*
> *Radiant flame of gold. . . .*
> *Every day and every night*
> *That I say the genealogy of Bride,*

I shall not be killed, I shall not be harried,
I shall not be put in a cell, I shall not be wounded,
Neither shall Christ leave me forgotten.
No fire, no sun, no moon will burn me,
No lake, no water, no sea shall drown me,
No arrow of fairy nor dart of fay shall wound me,
And I under the protection of my holy mother Mary,
And her under her gentle foster-mother, my beloved Bride.

—Martyrology of Donegal

Saint Brigid as a Child and Young Woman

As a child, Brigid was pious and generous. Ordered to churn butter by her master, she gave most of it away to the poor. When the magician scolded her, she prayed to heaven and suddenly the churn overflowed with butter. One of her biographers says ". . . The Magitian was so much astonished and moved, that he believed in Christ, setting both her and her mother at liberty."[58]

She was apparently great friends with Saint Patrick. *The Book of Armagh*, an eighth-century document, says that "Between Saint Patrick and Saint Brigid, the columns of the Irish, there was so great a friendship of charity that they had but one heart and one mind. Through him and through her Christ performed many miracles."

As a young woman she showed no interest in marriage, but seemed destined for a religious life. She refused many offers from local suitors. When her relatives became insistent, she plucked out her own eye; thus disfigured, she was no longer marriageable. Her shocked family relented, she replaced her eye, and it miraculously healed. Brigid soon became the first nun in Ireland. Saint Mel of Armagh is believed to have conferred abbatial authority on her; that is, made her an archbishop with the authority to appoint bishops and ordain priests. Some have found it surprising that a woman could have received such power from what today is a patriarchal church, but Brigid was part of a culture where noblewomen (her father *was* a king) and religious women could achieve great status.

Her Vocation in the Church

Brigid began her religious life humbly, however. Some say she created a tiny community with seven other virgins at Croghan Hill, which they later moved to the plains of Magh Life. Sometime between 470 and 490, she built for herself a little cell under an oak tree, and either brought her companions along or lived there alone until other women came to join her. The place was called Cill-Dara or *Kildara*, "the cell of the oak." Legend says that particular tree, "a very high oak tree which Brigid loved much, and blessed"[59] was especially sacred to the Druids. Under Brigid's leadership, the tiny community grew to become a great nunnery and monastery, and a famous center of learning, the first in Ireland. Around it grew up the cathedral city of Kildare. She asked Bishop Conleth to help her manage the abbey: "Thus, for centuries, Kildare was ruled by a double line of abbot-bishops and of abbesses, the Abbess of Kildare being regarded as superioress general of the convents in Ireland."[60]

Some people today believe that she had an intimate relationship with Bishop Conleth, but that notion was not endorsed by anyone in the centuries immediately following her life. On the other hand, *The Book of Invasions of Ireland* says candidly that Brigid had a female pupil named Darlugdacha who used to sleep with her.[61] Such close friendships were not unknown in convents. In his book Celtic Women, Peter Ellis adds that "Darlughdacha, who became abbess of Kildare on Brigid's death, means 'daughter of Lugh' and the 'saints lists' also give her feastday as 1st February."[62] However, Darlughdacha might actually be the original name for the goddess Brigit, especially since Brigit (Exalted One) is a title rather than a name.[63]

Hilaire Wood points out that:

> Whatever the truth of Brigid's private life, what is interesting here
> is her universality and the way that people . . . read into the sto-
> ries things about her with which they may identify. . . . A lover of
> women, a strong single woman, a woman in happy and fruitful
> relationship with a man—she becomes all things to all women.[64]

We may never know the truth of her personal life, but she certainly flourished in her vocation. In addition to governing a great abbey and directing charities for the poor, she founded a school of art at Kildare. The program included metalwork—indeed, there is a tradition that only working goldsmiths could be appointed as bishops!—and a scriptorium which produced famous illuminated manuscripts, including the glorious *Book of Kildare*, now lost.

However, Brigid was more than an artist and giver of alms. The white-cloaked saint's career had a decidedly feminist twist, according to journalist Helen O'Neill. "She rescued a young nun in trouble, miraculously causing an unwanted pregnancy to disappear. She freed slave women from their masters. She championed wives seeking divorce. Beautiful, powerful and brave, Bridget could also whip up a wicked home-brew."[65]

Her Death and Relics

Brigid died at Kildare on February 1 at about seventy-four, or some say eighty-eight, years of age. According to *The Martyrology of Donegal,* "The sacred virgin having run out the course of her mortall dayes, in the exercise of all kind of sanctimony, and innocency of life . . . [she] gave up her soule. . . . Her venerable body, was placed in a sumptuous monument of gould, and silver, adorned with jewells, and pretious stones, and was first interred in her owne monasterie at Kildare. . . ."

Three and a half centuries later, Viking raids made Kildare a dangerous place; and about 878, her bones were taken to Downpatrick, where they were placed in the tomb of Saint Patrick and Saint Columba. It seems that all the bodies were lost, for the chronicles say they were rediscovered in 1185 and then moved to Downpatrick Cathedral, attended by great pomp and circumstance.[66] During the reign of Henry VIII the monument of the three great saints was destroyed.

Her miraculous healing mantle is reputedly still at a church in Belgium; and a piece of her shoe resides in Dublin at the National Museum. Some of the saint's relics made their way back to Armagh, others to Scotland, Portugal, and Germany.[67]

It seems that, like many saints, her mortal remains traveled farther in death than she ever had during her life.

Many daughter convents sprang from Brigid's first, all across Ireland. Today in Kildare, the Round Tower stands at the original site of Brigid's convent and monastery. She has become known as the patron saint of Ireland and Irish nuns, New Zealand, mediation or peace-making, travelers, poets, dairymaids and cattle, blacksmiths, healers, fugitives, midwives, newborn babies, and scribes and calligraphers. ("Adjuva Brigitta, the Gaelic scribes wrote at the head of their manuscripts, 'O Brigid help me!' ")[68]

Tales of Saint Brigid

Most of Saint Brigid's biographies focus on various "wonder tales," for she had "wrought miracles more numerous than the sea-sands or the stars of Heaven. . . ."[69] Some of these may be goddess myths recycled by the Church or Irish authors. Unless otherwise attributed, the following stories are adapted from the *Martyrology of Donegal, A Calendar of the Saints of Ireland*, and *A Book of Saints and Wonders Put Down Here by Lady Gregory According to the Old Writings and the Memory of the People of Ireland*, by Lady Augusta Gregory.

Many tales emphasize Brigid's ability to feed people; they are reminiscent of Jesus' miracle of the loaves and fishes. But if "Saint" Brigid is really the daughter of the Dagda, the Celtic God of Abundance with the ever-filled cauldron, she was simply following in the family tradition. Other stories show her great love for animals, and a few reveal her sterner side.

Milk and Butter

An early legend tells that the child Brigid was sent to help the dairymaids with the milking; the milk would be churned into butter for the household. Brigid dutifully milked her share of cows, and then gave away all her milk to poor people living nearby. Well, the other maids had plenty of milk, so perhaps her mother let it go. But then the dairymaids began making butter, and young Brigid prayed for abundance. Lo and behold, the butter increased to twice as much as they could have expected! Brigid promptly took the extra butter and gave that to the poor as well.[70]

Another time some seven "venerable Bishops" were coming to visit Brigid. Brigid's cook, a woman with the memorable name "Blathnet," said they had no refreshment to offer the holy men. But three times in the same day Brigid was able to milk her cows, and each time they gave three times the normal amount of milk, until finally all the pails of Leinster overflowed and created what is still called the Lake of Milk.

Her Father's Sword

When Brigid had grown to young womanhood she returned to her father's house, where her generosity to the poor soon drove him to distraction. Though Brigid was his daughter, she was still a slave, and the chieftain finally decided to take drastic action. He resolved to sell her to King Dunlang of Leinster, and traveled with her to the royal stronghold.

When they arrived, her father told her to stay in the chariot while he went inside to speak to the king. As Brigid waited, a leper wandered by, begging alms. Brigid immediately handed him the only thing at hand—her father's fine sword. The surprised beggar did not stop to question his good fortune, but disappeared into the marketplace crowds with amazing speed.

Inside, Dubthach was complaining to the king about Brigid: "Nothing will stop her from selling my goods and giving to the poor!" Then he went out to the chariot to fetch her inside, and found his sword gone. His reaction is not recorded; though we can imagine the servants being startled as some very colorful language rang through the courtyard.

Inside, the king shrewdly asked Brigid: "If you came to be my bond-maid, how much of my wealth and cattle would you give away?" She was honest: "Jesus knows that if I had your wealth, I would give it all."

A little nonplused, but impressed by Brigid's charity, the king praised her to her father, then told him to set her free. King Dunlang did not, however, invite Brigid to stay at his house.

The Bishop's Robes

The king's caution was justified. Brigid was ever generous to the poor, and would give them the shirt off her back—or anyone else's back for that matter. Once she gave away Bishop Conleth's "very pretious, and rich garmentes"—his episcopal robes—to the poor. Luckily, within the same hour new ones of the same design, texture, and color were miraculously brought to her "in a waggon of two horses."

The nun's generosity is not quite so extreme a habit as it seems. Among Celtic peoples, it was customary for the nobility to exchange and circulate rich gifts among their families. What was noteworthy about Saint Brigid was that she distributed the largesse among the poor as well as the wealthy. In this, she is not so different from the later Saxon mythical hero, Robin Hood.

A Miracle for a Doge

Brigid was boiling some bacon for prestigious guests, when a hungry and miserable dog "did fawne upon her for meate." Naturally Brigid could not refuse the poor animal, so she cut off a chunk and gave "the doge" a piece . . . and then another . . . and another. When she later served her guests, the meat was whole, as though nothing had been cut from it. The high personages who were visiting witnessed the miracle, and declared they were not worthy to eat the sacred meat so it was given to the poor.

A Calf and a Loom Returned

Once Brigid was "benighted" (caught traveling at nightfall) and lodged with a poor woman, who was so determined to be a good hostess that she killed her only calf, and broke up her weaving loom to make a fire for cooking it. (Hospitality was very important to the Irish.) When Brigid discovered the extremes to which her hostess had gone, she vowed to reward the woman for her generosity. In the morning when Brigid left, the lady of the house discovered that both calf and loom had been replaced.

Beer for Easter

Christian holy days were celebrated a little differently in the fifth century; Irish congregations thought that serving beer at mass was a great idea. In preparation for Easter services, Saint Brigid volunteered to make the beverage. She had on hand "one onely measure or peck of malt," yet miraculously the quantity was sufficient to serve the congregations of eighteen churches for eight days. Another story says Brigid's bath water turned to beer, so perhaps she spent a lot of time in the tub that spring. The "beer" referred to was not very like our modern beers; it more closely resembled what we would call ale. But there were no complaints from the parishioners.

The legends imply that the saint was no teetotaler, and that she enjoyed a good brew. She once wished for "a great lake of ale for the King of Kings; I would wish the family of Heaven to be drinking it through life and time."

Her Cloak on a Sunbeam

Once during a "wet and moistey season" she was feeding her flock in a distant field, and was caught by a rain shower that soaked her to the skin. When she finally arrived home in her sopping cloak, "the quickness of her eyes being hindered" by water streaming down her face, she mistook a sunbeam for a pole or railing and threw her cloak on it to dry. Amazingly, the beam of light supported the wet cloak. A bishop who observed the incident—some say it was the famous Saint Brendan the Navigator—was highly impressed. His servant immediately cast the bishop's soggy cloak on to the sunbeam, whereupon it fell to the floor in a puddle.

A Way with Animals

Brigid could command ducks to come to her, which they would do "in great haste with prompt obedience." (Try it. It's not as easy as it sounds.) Then "the blessed virgin touched them gently and embrased them sweetly. . . ." and permitted them to fly away. Her skills were not limited to ducks; she could get songbirds to perch on her hand, and then ". . . she would stroke their heads with one finger, and laugh and talk to them; and when she told them to fly away again, they circled about her, singing for joy."[72]

Pigs were not exempt from her charms: once a "whild bore" came charging into the monastery courtyard, hotly pursued by hunters. The horsemen pulled up outside the gate and waited for the nuns to drive it out so they could kill it.

However, the law in those days was that any criminal could seek sanctuary on sacred ground. Brigid felt sorry for the exhausted beast and sent word to the hunters that the boar claimed right of sanctuary. They shouted in amazement, and milled around, complaining loudly that it was just an animal and pigs didn't have rights; but Brigid stuck to her word, and eventually the hunters rode off.

Meanwhile Brigid blessed the frightened boar and gave it water, and it remained tamely with the herd of monastery swine for the rest of its life. The "whild bore" later was enshrined in legend as Triath Torc, the King of the Boars.[73]

The Naked Cattle Rustlers

A farmer and his family came to celebrate a feast with Saint Brigid, and while they were away from home, thieves stole all their cattle. (Cattle raids were common in ancient Ireland, and those who really excelled at it were immortalized in epic poems.)

The escaping rustlers came to a flooded river and were determined to swim the cows across; but first the men took off their clothes and weapons to keep them dry, and tied them atop the animals. Halfway across the river, somehow knowing that Brigid would help them, the uncooperative cattle suddenly turned back and stampeded all the way to Brigid's home, "the men being stark naked following them." Brigid and her guests were waiting outside. Upon being caught red-handed, and doubtless red-faced as well, the thieves did penance at the monastery.

They got off lightly. Miranda Green mentions that Brigid "was a protector of cattle and was reputed to inflict such savage punishments as drowning or scalding upon anyone who dared steal her cows."[74]

The King's Fox

Once a simple country man came to the court of the King of Leinster, and there saw a fox running tame in the castle. Being less than bright and used to hunting such creatures, the bumpkin killed the fox. Unfortunately for him, the animal was the king's own pet, a marvelous trained fox that could perform "many trickes, and subtill feates." The enraged king threw the peasant in prison and threatened him with death, unless he could replace the fox. Not an easy task, especially if you're chained in a dungeon.

Saint Brigid heard of the man's plight and immediately set out for the king's court to plead for mercy. Along the way, a fox jumped into her coach and sat

quietly by her side. She presented it to the king, and amazingly, it performed all the same tricks as its predecessor. The king, mollified, released the repentant fox murderer to the bosom of his family, and Brigid returned to her monastery.

But the story does not end there. As soon as the country fellow and the saint were both well clear of the castle, the new fox ran away—pursued by an angry king, the army of Leinster, and a multitude of yelling courtiers, "footmen and horsemen and hounds"—none of whom were as fast as the fox, which reached its den and lived happily ever after.

The Friendly Fish

In the west of Ireland near the sea was a well sacred to Brigid, where dwelt a tiny fish. It was said the fish could be seen only once every seven years, and that whoever saw it would instantly be healed of any disease. An old woman tells of her visit to the well to cure an eye problem: ". . . I saw a little fish no longer than your finger . . . it was very civil coming hither to me and very pleasant wagging its tail. And it stopped and looked up at me and gave three wags of its back, and walked off again and went under the stone." None of the other people in the crowd glimpsed it. "It was no common fish. . . . It was surely Saint Brigid I saw that time; who else would it be?" Who else indeed? Within three days, the old woman's eye was healed.

Brigid Spreads Her Cloak

Brigid had strong opinions about the duty of the wealthy to aid the poor, and frequently asked the King of Leinster to contribute to her charities. When he proved to be tight with the royal pursestrings, she asked him at least to give her as much land as she could cover with her cloak, so that she could build her abbey. Thinking it a joke, he agreed.

Then four of Brigid's maidens came forth and took the corners of her cloak; facing the cardinal points of the compass, they began to run, and the cloak expanded. Other women grabbed the edges and joined the fun, and soon the cloak had grown to cover land a mile or more across.

The king was understandably alarmed, and Brigid calmly explained that "I am—or rather my cloak is—about to cover your whole province to punish you for your stinginess to the poor." The king quickly promised to give her a goodly acreage, if Brigid would call off her women. She agreed, and the king was far more willing to bring out his royal checkbook after that day.

The Apples and the Lepers

Brigid was not all sweetness and light. One day a woman brought some apples to Saint Brigid, and as it happened, some lepers were there begging alms of the saint. Brigid, generous as always to those in need, immediately proposed that the apples be shared with the lepers. However the woman took the apples away, saying, "I brought these apples for your selfe, and your virgins and not to be given to leapers."

The saint was offended by the lady's attitude, and told her that henceforth her trees would never bear fruit. Upon returning to her orchard, which had been heavy with apples, the woman found none at all, and indeed the trees remained barren ever after.

The Selfish Leper

Two lepers heard of the saint's marvelous healing skills, and came to her to be cured. She blessed some water and commanded them to wash each other with it. The first to be washed was suddenly healed, and gave thanks; and Brigid said, "Wash now your fellow." But the former leper, now healthy and clean, refused to touch his old comrade. Either God or Brigid applied sudden justice, for then he immediately exclaimed, "I feel sparkles of fire upon my shoulders," and his body was instantly covered again with leprosy—while his unwashed companion was healed.

Saint Brigid, Jesus, and Mary

In Christian legend, Saint Brigid is regarded as the midwife who assisted at Jesus' birth. Yes, she was born some four centuries after the event, but religious legends need not conform to historical timelines. Perhaps because Brigit the goddess ruled healing and childbirth, she was a natural choice for midwife; and perhaps in a mystical sense she *was* present.

According to another legend, Brigid later saved Jesus and Mary from the wrath of King Herod. They were escaping to Egypt when Herod's soldiers caught up with them. Brigid placed a crown of candles on her head and danced across the dunes, leading the pursuers away.

Even more importantly, Saint Brigid was extolled as Jesus' foster-mother. To understand how significant that is, one must remember that among noble Celtic families, children were often fostered to other households or courts at an early age. This may have been done to strengthen connections between ruling families and to ensure peace; if your own child was essentially a hostage at another chieftain's household, it was unlikely you would call out the army over a land dispute.

In any case, the children developed close bonds with the foster families where they spent their childhood and adolescent years. To the Celts, a foster mother was in some ways more important in a child's life than its birth mother. For the Irish to assign Brigid the role of Jesus' foster-mother was to give her incredible status. The Vatican, probably ignorant of Celtic customs, may have paid little attention to the foster mother phenomenon; but to the Irish, Brigid became "The Mary of the Gaels" and a primary figure in the Holy Family.

Saint Brigid's Goddess Connections

Several authors simply assert that Saint Brigid was not a real person, but simply a Celtic goddess recycled by Christian missionaries to make the new faith more palatable to the conservative country folk of Ireland. The fabulous tales which fill her biographies may have been lifted from the oral mythology of a deity.

"Finding the cult of Brigid impossible to eradicate, the Catholic Church rather unwisely canonized her as a saint . . ." says Barbara Walker. "[Her] convent at Kildare . . . was known for its heathenish miracles and evidences of fertility magic. Cows never went dry; flowers and shamrocks sprang up in Brigid's footprints; eternal spring reigned in her bower. Irish writers refused to reduce their goddess to mere sainthood, and insisted that she was Queen of Heaven, which meant identifying her with Mary."[76]

Those who suggest that Saint Brigid was simply a reworked goddess have a strong case. Even as a child she had godlike powers. The folk tales attribute these to the Christian god, suggesting that Brigid was so devoted that God refused her nothing. However, they are the sort of miracles that can just as easily be attributed to a goddess acting on her own initiative.

Brigid founded her monastery at "Cill-Dara," under an oak tree sacred to the goddess-worshipping Druids, whose name translates as "oak-seers." She appointed goldsmiths to be bishops; an odd custom for a Christian ecclesiastic, but not so strange if ordained by the Goddess of Smithcraft. During her long ministry Saint Brigid was renowned for her healing powers, just as the deity Brigit was Goddess of Healing. The saint founded a school of art that produced beautiful calligraphy; here we find echoes of the Goddess of Inspiration. In short, almost every attribute of the goddess appears again in the saint's story.

Saint Brigid was closely associated with fire, and had an "eternal flame" at her shrine. This flame was reminiscent of the sacred fire at the temple of Vesta in Rome, or that of Minerva's sanctuary in Britain at Aquae Sulis. According to legend, nineteen virgins tended the flame in turn, but on the twentieth day of each

cycle Brigid herself watched the fire. She was herself identified with fire: the hymn *Brigit Be Bithmaith* says "Brigid, excellent woman, sudden flame, golden, sparkling, may she bear us to the eternal kingdom, She the sun, fiery, radiant!"[77]

There are many Pagan fire and sun goddesses, from Amaterasu of Japan to Bast and Sekhmet of Egypt. However, fire has never been an especially powerful symbol in Christianity—possibly because the early Church fathers wanted to distance themselves from the Pagan religions that used it so lavishly. While the Pagans were building their immemorial bonfires on the hilltops, the followers of Jesus were immersing themselves in rivers, in the rite of baptism.

Why then, does fire figure so prominently in the story of an Irish saint? At least one Church father felt it was all too Pagan; in 1220 C.E., Bishop Henry de Londres of Dublin ". . . was incensed. He . . . decreed that the keeping of the eternal flame was a Pagan custom and ordered the sacred flame to be extinguished."[78]

Soon the flame was lit again, and maintained until the reign of Henry VIII (1509–1541) and the Reformation, when the monastery was destroyed and the flame extinguished once more. In modern times it was lit once more, by Sister Mary Minehan of the Order of Brigandine Nuns, and it burns today in Kildare.

Another hint of the saint's goddess roots comes from *The Martyrology of Donegal*; here is the charm in which, under Saint Brigid's protection, "No fire, no sun, no moon will burn me." This is a natural enough function for a goddess who controlled the fiery realms. She is then invoked as a protection against drowning; for a goddess of sacred springs and wells, for whom rivers are named, this too is logical.

Saint Brigid was connected with beer or ale, and in Irish tradition, drinking is related to poetic inspiration, and to the conferring of sovereignty. Coronation ceremonies involved the drinking of red ale, possibly as a symbolic union with the "blood" of the land. Inspiration and the confirmation of rulership were two of the functions of Brigit the goddess.

The Saint's Faery Connections

There are other clues that the saint was more than she seemed. Her possible birthplace of Faughart was associated with the legends of Queen Meave or Medb ("She who intoxicates") of Connacht—Queen Mab of the Faery people? Later Saint Brigid did missionary work there, founding several churches in the Diocese of Elphim; note that the Land of Faery is called Elphame ("elf-home") in many legends. Further, Brigid could protect people from the otherworldly powers; "No dart of fairy nor arrow of fay will wound me. . . ." What better source of protection than a Queen of Faery Herself?

As mentioned earlier, the faery folk or Sidhe lived in the earth under magickal hills. A Scottish rhyme about the Feast Day of Bride begins: "*This is the day of Bride, The queen will come from the mound. . . .*"[79] What would a Christian saint be doing anywhere near a fairy mound? In other versions it is a "serpent" that will emerge from a hole; is Bride equated with a serpent? That would be natural enough for a deity, since the serpent symbolizes the goddess in many cultures.

Saint Brigid: A Real Person?

Brigid seems to dwell somewhere between myth and reality. Her historical status may never be known. The biographies left by pious Irish monks are unconvincing; none of them were written until long after the latest reported date for Brigid's death. There is room here for innocent error or even fraud. Of course there are the relics . . . which according to legend were removed from Kildare, lost for a couple of centuries, found again, and moved again. As far as we know, there has never been a scientific study of these or the other scattered relics attributed to her; they might belong to anyone.

Interestingly, the goddess Brigit had a sacred grove at Derry Down, near the cathedral where Brigid is said to be interred. The mystery is deepened by Barbara Walker's provocative comments about Patrick: "An old distich said, 'On the hill of Down, buried in one tomb, were Bridget and Patricius.' Since Patrick's name meant 'father,' and he was as apocryphal as other Irish saints, he may have been a new name for Brigit's old consort the Dagda or 'father.'"[80]

Was Brigit a goddess, or a human woman, or both? It is entirely possible that a nun named for the goddess lived in the fifth and sixth centuries, ministered to the poor, and founded the abbey at Kildare. After her death, natural confusion might have credited her with the wondrous feats of the Celtic goddess for whom the nun was named. Or the Roman hierarchy may have campaigned to transfer the goddess' attributes—and her Pagan following—to the woman who was, so we are told, an obedient servant of the Church. As Saint Ultan rhapsodizes, "In our island of Hibernia Christ was made known to man by the very great miracles which he performed through the happy virgin. . . ."[81] It would not be the first time that Rome enlisted the memory of a Pagan deity for its own purposes.

In the end, it may not matter. Whether or not she ever walked the earth, her reality as a spiritual and emotional force is undeniable.

Conclusion: The Humanization of Brigit and Her Meaning Today

As a goddess, Brigit teaches important lessons. Too often we remember only goddesses of spring and summer, of flowers and warm sunlight. Brigit reminds us that the strength of women is also manifest as the invincible fire that burns steadily through the heart of winter, no matter how dark and cold the world. And she is special not only to women generally, but to all poets and artists, healers and midwives, herbalists and farmers and gardeners, warriors and rulers, and craftspeople of all kinds.

And yet, exalted as the goddess was among the ancient Celts, it would seem that her apparent demotion to human saint has not harmed her reputation at all. "In Ireland to-day, after 1500 years, the memory of [Brigid] is as dear as ever to the Irish heart. . . ."[82]

Gods and goddesses are well and good, but they tend to be awesome and remote beings. By definition they exist beyond the world of humanity, and it is rather challenging to see them as role models or confidants. Christianity has addressed this problem with Jesus, a god who became human and walked among us; and with Mary, a woman caught up in divine events. Both are bridges between human and divine, and are easier to relate to than a god who created the heavens and the earth and spoke in a voice of thunder.

Ironically, the Catholic Church's apparent reconstruction of Brigit may have had the unintended effect of making female divinity more accessible. Saint Brigid may have done for the Goddess what Jesus did for Jehovah. Where once Brigit was the exalted bestower of sovereignty, the goddess of the sun, and the power of rushing rivers, she has become—a woman. A milkmaid, even; a farm girl who tended sheep and got drenched in rainstorms and gave butter to poor people . . . and grew up to found a great abbey. A warm and compassionate person, who had an iron will and a quick temper, who argued with kings, and loved art, and liked her beer. Brigid the woman could be a big sister, a beloved aunt, a heroine, and a role model. She could be a friend.

Notes

The *Book of Lismore* and the *Martyrdom of Donegal* are ancient texts, quoted on many modern websites.

1. Brighid's Academy of Healing Arts website.

2. Monaghan, *New Book of Goddesses & Heroines*, p. 74.

3. Among the few sources that mention the goddess are the *Lebor Gabála Erenn*, a blend of history and Celtic mythology from medieval times, and Cormac mac Cuilennáin's *Sanas Chormaic*, written about 900 C.E. Tina Deegan, "Historical Background on 'The Exalted One,'" Shrine of the Goddess Brighid website. (Shrine website.)

4. "Saint Brigid: The Mary of the Gael," Catholic Information Network website. (CIN website.)

5. Ibid.

6. Walker, *Women's Encyclopedia of Myths and Secrets*, "Brigit, Saint."

7. Fiona Macleod, *Winged Destiny*.

8. MacAnTsaoir, "Imbolc—Brigit's Festival," in Daughters of the Flame website.

9. ADF website.

10. Liafal, "Brigid: Flame of Two Eternities," in ADF website.

11. Ibid.

12. Ibid.

13. Donncha, Dennis King quoted in "Brigit, Bright Goddess of the Gael" in Imbas website.

14. Green, *Celtic Goddesses,* p. 198.

15. MacLeod, op.cit.

16. L. MacDonald, "Celtic Folklore: The People of the Mounds—Articles on The Sidhe," *Dalriada Magazine* in ShadowNet website.

17. Sacred Source website.

18. Green, p. 106.

19. Campanelli, *Ancient Ways*, p. 14.

20. "The Goddess Brigit," *The Sweetgrass Times*.

21. Campanelli, p. 14.

22. Gregory, Lady Augusta. *A Book of Saints and Wonders Put Down Here by Lady Gregory According to the Old Writings and the Memory of the People of Ireland.*

23. Chalice Center website.

24. Monaghan, p. 74.

25. Campanelli, p. 11.

26. Shrine website.

27. CCL

28. Brighid's Academy of Healing Arts website.

29. Lafferty, Ann. "Imbolc." *EarthSpirit* newsletter.

30. Brighid's Academy of Healing Arts website.

31. Lisa Spindler, "Brigid," Encyclopedia Mythica website.

32. Liafal at ADF website.

33. Chalice Center website.

34. Beane and Doty, *Myths, Rites, Symbols*, p. 429.

35. Walker, op cit.

36. Shrine website.

37. Chalice Center website.

38. Shrine website.

39. Liafal at ADF website.

40. Monaghan, p. 74.

41. "The Goddess Brigit," *The Sweetgrass Times.*

42. Sacred Source website.

43. Walker, op. cit.

44. ShadowNet website.

45. Ibid.

46. Ibid.

47. Carmichael, Alexander. *Carmina Gadelica.*

48. ShadowNet website.

49. Ibid.

50. "A Timeline of Irish History," Clannada na Gadelica website.

51. Powell, p. 57.

52. Powell, *The Celts,* p. 56.

53. "Scandinavian Dublin," indiao.ie/~kfinlay/ossory/ossory1.htm.

Chapter 2

54. Powell, pp. 97–98.

55. "Saint Brigid: The Mary of the Gael," Catholic Information Network website.

56. The *Catholic Encyclopedia* online, and *Historia Brittonum, Excerpts from the Welsh Latin, History of Britons*, trans. Pamela Hopkins and J.T. Koch).

57. CIN website.

58. *Martyrology of Donegal.*

59. CIN website.

60. *Catholic Encyclopedia* online.

61. Condren, *Goddess and the Serpent,* p. 71.

62. Ellis, Peter, *Celtic Women,* quoted in Brigit, Bright Goddess of the Gael website.

63. Condren, p. 71.

64. Brigit's Forge website.

65. "Bridget's Legacy," Helen O'Neill, Ord Brigideach website.

66. *Catholic Encyclopedia* online.

67. CIN website, and "Brigid of Kildare," For All the Saints website.

68. CIN website.

69. CIN website.

70. Manning-Sanders, *Festivals,* p. 38.

71. CIN website.

72. Manning-Sanders, p. 38.

73. For All the Saints website.

74. Green, *Celtic Goddesses,* p. 200.

75. McGarry, "St. Brigid's Cloak," *Great Folk Tales of Old Ireland,* p.97.

76. Graves, *White Goddess,* p.144, quoted within Walker, *Women's Encyclopedia of Myths and Secrets,* "Brigit, Saint."

77. Brigit's Forge website.

78. Daughters of the Flame website.

79 Chalice Center website.

80. Walker, op. cit.

81. *Catholic Encyclopedia* online.

82. Ibid.

Customs, Traditions, and Symbols

Customs and traditions are far more than habits handed down through the years. They add meaning to our lives in many ways. They mark our place in the cycle of the seasons, reminding us where we have come from and what lies ahead. They personalize the great forces of Nature, such as fire and fertility, and also the intangibles like inspiration or sovereignty. They help us understand the mysteries of life by explaining them in parables or linking them to concrete symbols. They conserve our culture and, therefore, our values from generation to generation. The customs, traditions, and symbols discussed here can enrich your life—or at the very least, provide some fond memories in years to come.

A Welcoming Ritual

A little ritual is still used to welcome Brigit (and therefore spring) in many Celtic homes. A member of the family goes out to gather the rushes for making Brigit's crosses. When they return, they cover their head and knock at the door. Someone opens the door, and the woman of the house (*Bean an Tighe*) greets the family member "Welcome, Brigit" (*Fáilte leat a Bhríd*), to which the stand-in for Brigit replies "God bless the people of this house" (*Beannacht Dé ar daoine an tighe seo*).[1]

As part of this ceremony, you might add this translation of a Scottish Gaelic invocation:

> *May Brigit give blessing to the house that is here;*
> *Brigit, the fair and tender . . .*
> *Rich-tressed maiden of ringlets of gold.*[2]

Once "Brigit" has offered her blessing, the evening's activities begin in earnest: the making of the Brigit's crosses, games, stories, divination, and feasting.

A Brigit Corn Dolly

A very old custom involves making a Brigit effigy or "corn dolly," that can either be taken around the village in processional, or placed in a "Bride's bed" to bring fertility and good fortune to the home—or both! In Scotland the doll is sometimes called a "biddy" (a nickname for Brigit) or *Brídeóg* ("breed-oge"), meaning "Little Bride."[3]

Note that corn dollies are not made of corn (or maize), as the term is used in North America. "Corn" to old Europeans meant any kind of common grain such as oats, rye, or wheat.

If you made a corn dolly at Lammas or Lughnassad the previous fall, then you may wish to simply re-use it, dressing it in white and red so that the Harvest Crone becomes the Spring Bride. Pauline Campanelli reports that ". . . at the time of the Autumnal Equinox, a bundle of grain or a bunch of corn was ritually brought into the house. In ancient times this would have been the last sheaf of wheat or the last row of corn . . . [where] the Spirit of the Grain or the Goddess

Herself . . . had retreated. [This handful of wheat straws, with grain still attached, is sometimes called 'the neck.'] This last sheaf of grain of the old harvest is then the seed of the next harvest. It is another link in the endless chain of immortality, the continuous cycle of birth, death, and rebirth."[4]

The grain bundle, often made into a human shape, is variously called the Corn or Barley Mother, the Sheaf Mother, or the Harvest Mother.

Some traditions prefer not to recycle the old corn dolly, but instead dispose of her in a ritual fire or as compost, and make a fresh figure for the Bride. Before disposing of the last sheaf, Scots farmers would attach it to the harnesses of their plow horses as they began to plow the fields for the new planting, "thus connecting the old cycle of growth and harvest with the new one."[5]

Should you choose to make a new figure, there are many different ways to do it. The body can simply be a sheaf of oats with a crosspiece to make the arms, as is often used in Scotland. It could be an ear of maize. You could also use a Brigit's Cross woven of rushes, as is done in the Hebrides Islands.

A mat may be woven of straw or other grain, then rolled and tied into a cylindrical dolly with three ribbons to represent the Triple Goddess. Alternatively, you can make a more complex dolly by tying sheaves around a small ball for the head, with a larger ball immediately below it for the torso, and then splitting the sheaves in two parts for the legs. The arms can be fastened on separately.[6]

If you braid or weave your dolly, start by choosing the best straws and soaking them in cool water, then wrapping them in a towel for a little while. This makes them more pliable and less likely to crack as you work.[7]

When the dolly is ready, dress her in white doll clothing, lace handkerchiefs, or white cloth and pieces of lace from the fabric store, with whatever ribbons and jewelry you want to add. You can make her outfit very simple, but it may be more fun to see how fancy you can get. The more care and love you put into the doll, the more Brigit will be pleased when she visits!

Traditionally a sparkling crystal or colored shell is placed over the figure's heart to represent the star over Bethlehem that led Brigid to the baby Jesus. This adornment is called the "Guiding Star of Brigid," or *reul-iuil-Bride*.

When the holiday is past, you can find a place of honor for the dolly on your front door or on your mantle. She will serve as a talisman to protect your home and bring prosperity and good fortune for the coming year. Greet her periodically and ask her blessing when you especially need it. In the autumn, between Samhain and Yule, you should return the dolly (without her finery) to field or forest, or use her to feed wild birds during the winter's cold.[8]

Brigit's Bed

The goddess Brigit is not some distant deity who is never seen by the people who worship her. In fact, on her special day she may even come around to your home and spend the night. To show your hospitality, create a "Brigit's Bed" (*leaba Bride*) near the hearthfire. This is the warmest and comfiest spot in the cottage for a weary traveler, all the better if there is a cauldron filled with hearty mutton stew simmering over the coals on an iron hook—a welcome snack for the guest who wakens to its rich aroma in the middle of the night!

By inviting Brigit to stay overnight in your home, you are symbolically asking that her powers of fertility, blessing, and healing be with your family all year long, so it's important that you make your home—and Brigit's bed—as attractive as you possibly can!

This means cleaning your house thoroughly (see Chapter 5), then decorating it with candles, ribbons, and flowers; and of course, filling it with all the savory smells of your feast. What goddess could resist dropping by?

The "bed" can be anything large enough to hold the Brigit doll you will make. A child's cradle is fine, or perhaps a large basket or wooden box with a folded blanket or some thick towels inside.

If you wish, you can make a full-sized bed near the fire just as you might for any of your friends invited to stay the night. As an alternative to making a corn dolly "Brigit," take a broom and tie a red kerchief around her "head." The broom is an old, old symbol of female power and fertility. In England of centuries past, the words "broom" and "besom" could refer to a woman or to certain parts of her body that are directly related to sex and procreation.

You don't want Brigit to be lonely in her bed, so next to her place a beribboned fruitwood wand with a pinecone attached to the end. This represents the god—whichever one Brigit would enjoy having next to her. This is especially important if your family is hoping for a fertile year—more children, livestock, crops, money, or whatever your family wants to increase.

Some sources bluntly call the god-wand a "phallic wand"[9] or "Priapic wand," but others are a bit more refined: "In her hand they placed a small straight white wand, generally of birch, the tree of spring, or other sacred wood: straight to signify justice, white for purity and peace."[10]

For stronger fertility magick, place the wand across the doll in an "X" shape, forming the Norse rune *Gifu*, which means "gift." If you are really serious about fertility, you can throw some nuts—male fertility symbols—into the bed as well.[11]

Later in the evening, you may want to gather by Bride's Bed and call the ancient greeting three times: "Brid is come, Brid is welcome!" Sing songs, tell the old legends, toast her health, and perhaps leave a snack at the front door. Then retire to your own beds, but leave candles burning throughout the night. (In the interest of safety, use either a long-burning votive candle in glass or a large, solid pillar candle, and place its holder on a dish, and that on a non-flammable surface out of reach of family pets.)

Or if you wish, an all-night vigil and meditation can be a profoundly spiritual experience. It's up to you whether you give Brigit and the god a little privacy to do fertility magick for you, or whether you want to meditate with her to seek her counsel on some other issue such as healing or inspiration.

The Hearthfire

The hearthfire, sacred to Brigit, was her altar in every home. Each family's hearth was the gathering place and heart of the home. Here food was prepared, and in the evening it was a major source of light and warmth. During long, cold winter nights, it was where fishing nets might be mended, wool carded and spun, or an orphaned lamb nursed along. Here also the storyteller, the *seannachaidh*, would tell rousing tales of gods and heroes, of great storms and long-ago battles, of fairy folk, leprechauns, and banshees.

Little wonder that every culture has its myths of a cunning hero, reckless trickster, or compassionate god who stole the secret of fire for humanity. When winter storms covered the land, a warm hearth was the difference between life and death. It was "the sun brought down to human level as the miraculous power of fire."[12]

At Imbolg or Candlemas, in the depth of winter, the fire was more important than ever. The fire was not allowed to go out, and was carefully fed with special kinds of wood on the eve of Brigit's visit. (You can use any kind of wood special to you. For protection, place a rowan twig in the very center of the flames.)

Each night the fire was "smoored" by the lady of the house, that is, covered carefully so that the coals would stay hot overnight and be easy to kindle the next morning. As she did so, she would ask Brigit's blessing and protection for home, family, and cattle:

> *. . . I will smoor the hearth*
> *As Brighid the Fostermother would smoor*
> *The Fostermother's holy name*
> *Be on the hearth, be on the herd*
> *Be on the household all."[13]*

In the morning as the householder rebuilt the fire, she would once again ask the protection of Mary and of "Saint Brigid, the radiant flame" herself:

> *I will build the hearth*
> *As Mary would build it.*
> *The encompassment of Bride and of Mary*

Guarding the hearth, guarding the floor,
Guarding the household all.[14]

If you have a fireplace or even a wood stove, there is no reason why you cannot resurrect these charming traditions, at least for the holiday season.

Making Brigit's Crosses or Sun Wheels

Brigit's Crosses, or Saint Brigid's Crosses, are a handicraft or art form woven of straw or rushes. The difference between a Brigit's Cross and certain types of corn dolly is a little hazy, and occasionally the terms are used interchangeably. Although some of the figures created are crosses, the custom is probably pre-Christian in origin; the crosses are equal-armed, and resemble solar symbols used by the Norse and other Pagan societies.

Sun symbols may have been a form of sympathetic magick, encouraging the sun to grow in strength and bring the spring. Janet and Stewart Farrar believe they were connected with ceremonies preparing seed grain for the spring planting. In either case, they were and are used as talismans to bring fertility, prosperity, and protection to the household.

The crosses would be created at Imbolg, sometimes on the evening of February 1. They were hung on the door or over it, near the hearth, under the eaves, or in the barn—anywhere that luck and protection were desired. Rhiannon Ryall says that "a pair of them were hung up

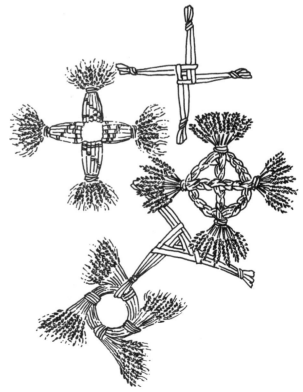

on the gable ends of houses as protective charms, by the men who thatched the roofs, one Dolly representing the God, the other the Goddess."[15]

The best-known Brigit's Cross is the simple equal-armed style with each arm offset at the center (see illustration, p. 67). There is also a Celtic Cross version, enclosed in a circle; a triskele or triskelion, which may represent Brigit's triple-goddess nature; and non-cruciform shapes such as the Tall Spiral, Love Token, Lover's Knot, and Welsh Fan.[16]

How are they made? Web author Hilaire Wood explains that "Traditionally the rushes were picked by hand, not cut, on 31st January, the night before Saint Brigit's Day. They were blessed and the crosses were made in a sunwise direction, from left to right."[17]

In Christian homes, holy water may be sprinkled on the rushes. Since water was sacred to the goddess Brigit, this would be a natural thing for Pagans to do as well. Even better, soak the rushes for a few minutes to get the dust off and make them pliable. Instructions are shown on page 69 for making a very simple form of Brigit's Cross. Still more methods are described on the Internet and in craft books. You can bury any leftover materials, or dispose of them in some other reverent way.

Making a Brigit's Cross*

1. Gather several pieces (9 or more) of rush or straw, about 8–12 inches long. (You can make the cross in any size, but this is a good size for beginners.) Soak the rushes for half an hour or until they are flexible. Meanwhile, get 4 rubber bands to hold the ends temporarily, and four pieces of string or ribbon to bind the ends permanently. You may also want some paint or clear coating to seal the cross after it is completed and dried.

2. Holding one straw vertical, wrap a second around it with the ends facing right.

3. Hold the center tightly and rotate it to the left. Fold a third straw over the second, to the right.

* Adapted from "How to Make a Traditional St. Brigit's Cross," www.geocities.com/RainForest/Vines/5863

4. Rotate it all left again, and fold a fourth straw tightly over both the third and first straws, to the right.

5. Continue by turning the cross left each time, and adding another straw around the vertical ones.

6. Keeping holding the center tightly as you turn and add new straws, until you have used them up.

7. Snug each straw in to the center. When all the straws are in place, fasten the ends.

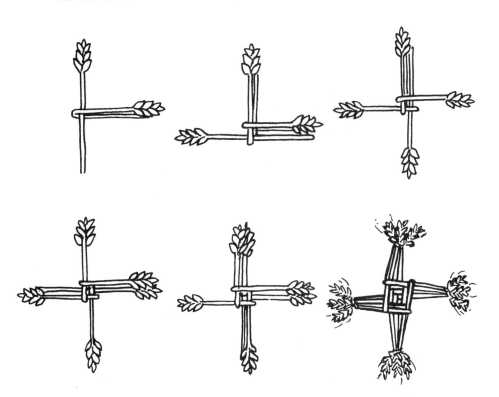

A Gift for Brigit

Remember leaving milk and cookies out for Santa on Christmas Eve? The custom probably came from Brigit's feast day, and she would probably appreciate it if you left less for the "jolly old elf" and remembered to leave something for her.

Apparently her tastes are simple. A loaf of bread and a jug of milk are quite sufficient. Cake would not be spurned. Even a piece of buttered bread on the churn is appreciated, since Brigit is the goddess who presides over the making of butter.[18] And don't forget to put a candle in the window, so she knows there's a snack waiting at your house.

Not all of the customary offerings are edible, at least after the householder is done with them: "Another ancient custom involved the throwing of a sheaf of oats or cake of bread against the doorstep on the eve of Imbolg to drive away hunger during the coming year."[19] Yet another tradition involves pouring milk on your threshold as a blessing or libation (preferably not when the neighbors are watching). You are certainly allowed to modify the custom and simply sprinkle a few drops.[20]

In a related custom, "Sometimes . . . a bundle of straw or fresh rushes were laid on the threshold for her to kneel upon to bless the house, or possibly so she—or the cow!—could wipe their feet before entering."[21] Cow? Yes. Legend says that Brigit travels with a white cow, so some hay, grass, or corn would be appropriate.

Begging for Biddy— "Alms for Poor Biddy"

In some areas, a procession of young people would accompany Brigit around the village on the evening of February 1, begging alms for "poor Biddy." Brigit might be enacted by a girl in costume, a doll clothed in bridal finery, or even a churn-dash covered in straw and decorated.[22]

If the group was composed of young girls, they would dress in white and often sing or dance as they went from house to house; they were known as the "Bride Maiden band," or *banal Bride*. In some villages boys would dress up in girls' clothes and go begging door-to-door; they were called the "Biddy boys."

Originally the idea was probably to imitate Brigit's own charity, collecting food and clothing for the poor. However, traditions transmute over time, and eventually the contributions were sought for Brigit herself. Patricia Monaghan says that in Kerry, on the southwest coast of Ireland, the children would sing:

Something for poor Biddy!
Her clothes are torn.
Her shoes are worn.
Something for poor Biddy![23]

Wherever the Biddy callers went, the householders would give gifts of flowers, cheese, eggs, butter, biscuits or bannocks, or money.[24] Unlike modern Halloween trick-or-treating, however, candy was rare; sugar was expensive. This generosity to Brigit was thought to encourage a bountiful harvest, prosperity, and good luck.

When the band of youngsters had completed the circuit through village or neighborhood:

> . . . the girls spent the night at a house where the [Biddy] figure was made to sit in state, while the girls prepared the Bride feast for the next day. The young men of the town soon came knocking at the door and were let in to pay tribute to Bride, after which there were songs, dancing and much merrymaking until the break of day. At first light, they all joined hands and sang a hymn to Bride, and shared out the remains of the feast among the poor women of the town.[25]

As a more compassionate variant on this custom, your family might invite an elderly woman to join your feast. She certainly won't put a damper on the young peoples' festivities, at least if she goes to bed as early as we do. Then again, she might surprise you and dance until dawn.

A Procession by Torchlight

It is easy to imagine girls and boys running through an Irish village, calling for "Alms for Biddy!" If you would like to share the fun in a slightly more formal way, make torches and have an evening parade in honor of the goddess Brigit. You could also use candles. Make simple but effective drip-catchers for the hot wax with circles of thin cardboard, cutting an "X" in the middle of each and pushing the candles halfway through. Participants hold the candles by the end under the cardboard.

With great ceremony, kindle the fire from which the torches and candles are lit. Do it in the old way, without matches or lighters. Instead, make a need-fire (from the Norse *nied-fyr,* or forced fire) during the day using a magnifying lens, or make one by night with either flint and steel or the bow-and-drill method. Books on wilderness survival will show you how.

A processional should involve costumes or at least festive dress, drumming and singing, and a destination. If you don't have a holy well in the neighborhood, you can always have a bonfire laid in an open area well away from buildings, and proceed there to light the fire. After a few songs, return indoors for the feast, leaving a couple of fire watchers to make sure it's out.

Another option is to circle your garden or fields with torches; widdershins (counterclockwise) to banish and purify, then again deosil (clockwise) to charge the soil with energy in readiness for planting.

The Crown of Lights

On Santa Lucia's Day, which falls near the Winter Solstice, a girl or young woman enters the festivities wearing a crown of candles. She is actually the Christianized version of Lucina, the Roman goddess of light, and the crown of lights is her halo. Brigit and Lucina may not be the same goddess, but they certainly had much in common—which may be why Brigit has adopted the crown in many modern ceremonies.

Edain McCoy suggests that originally the woman representing the goddess simply carried a ring of candles, which was "a lighted sun wheel, a symbol of the

Wheel of the Year being warmed and lighted again by the returning sun."[26] Later someone had the idea of wearing the ring on her head.

Today, the crowned person may be a little girl representing the new year; a woman acting the part of Lucina or Brigit; or the Mother Goddess who is quickened at Imbolg.[27] She may arrive at an outdoor assembly in a horse-drawn sleigh, as is common in Eastern Europe.[28] She can enter the ritual with her crown alight, or the lighting and coronation may be a central part of the ceremony.

The crown itself can be made from a holly wreath, or in the Swedish style using woven wortleberry twigs,[29] assuming you can find and identify a wortleberry bush. You might use a mix of winter evergreens and spring flowers to mark the changing of the season. The crown could also be decorated with non-flammable gold or silver garlands.

To make a wreath, begin with a circle of wire a little larger than your head. Around that, wrap straw or greenery, tying it on with red ribbons, spiraling around and around. Get a friend to help—with two hands it's nearly impossible, with four it's easy. As you go around, remember to leave spaces for the candles to stand up between the branches, or wrap the straw loosely so the candles can be worked in later. Make the wreath a big, puffy affair, so the candles have more purchase and will be more secure.

Tie off the ribbon in a big, showy bow with long streamers to hang down your back. Now put it on over a fireproof skullcap, and mold it to fit your head (that's what the wire is for; no one has a perfectly round head). Then have your friend put in candles at least four inches long, preferably red or white dripless tapers. Stick them in almost all the way through. Make sure the tapers are vertical while the wreath sits on your head at a slight tilt. While you are wearing the wreath with the tapers lit, be very aware of your surroundings; for instance, don't sit near draperies!

Janet and Stewart Farrar suggest a crown made with birthday candles and an aluminum-foil cap; or an electric crown, with small individual penlights or flashlight bulbs connected to a hidden battery pack. To update this, try a short length of tiny tree lights, or use the battery-operated candles now available. Perhaps simplest and safest of all, make a crown with many small mirrors from a craft store, which will catch the light and twinkle as you move your head.[30]

We suggest electric lights or mirrors, for safety reasons; but if you decide to go with candles, have them lit only for a brief time during the entrance or climax of the ceremony. Then discreetly extinguish the candles, or place the entire crown on a fireproof surface to continue burning.

Brigit's Mantle

We learned in the stories about Saint Brigit that she had a magickal mantle or cloak that could expand to cover many acres. The goddess had a cloak of green, the color associated with the Faery folk, but by the time she became a saint it had turned white. The "authentic, original" cloak preserved as a relic in Europe, however, is blue. In any case it had healing and protective powers.

Legend says that if you leave a bit of cloth outside on Saint Brigit's Eve, from sunset until dawn, she will bless it and give it the same powers as the original. It need not be a large or expensive piece of fabric; even a ribbon will do. Your cloth is known henceforth as "Brigid's mantle" or *brat Bhride*; keep it for a full year, then renew the blessing at Brigit's next visit. It is especially beneficial for sick animals; try it on your sheep or cows—or cat or dog.[31]

If you visit any of the wells or springs associated with Brigit, you may find strips of cloth tied to the trees and bushes nearby. No one knows whether this is a related custom, or an offering to the goddess, or a sort of prayer flag to flutter in the breeze and attract her attention to the owner's needs.

Brigit's Magickal Girdle

Brigit's girdle (the medieval word for belt) had the same healing powers. Hilaire Wood tells of a story in which Brigit actually gave the magickal item to a poor woman, who promptly went into business as a healer and was able to support herself with it. He goes on to describe a related holiday custom:

> The *Crios Bríde* was woven from straw at Imbolc and men and women would step through it three times, kissing it and stepping through it right foot first, as a symbolic act of rebirth in order to ensure health and protection for the year ahead. While doing so they recited the following:
>
> > *The Girdle, the girdle of Brigit, my Girdle,*
> > *The girdle of the four crosses,*
> > *Mary entered it, Brigit emerged from it;*
> > *If you be improved today,*
> > *May you be seven times better*
> > *A year from today.*[32]

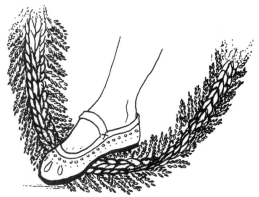

This may be the Christianized version of a far older Pagan charm. The girdle might have been pictured as a wide belt or sash with four crosses embroidered on it, which symbolized protection from danger at all four cardinal directions. The reference to "seven times better" may simply be a poetic way of saying *much* better, or it may be purposeful invocation of a lucky number sometimes connected with Faery.

Burning the Yule Greens

In *An ABC of Witchcraft Past and Present*, Doreen Valiente says, "The evergreens for Yuletide decorations were holly, ivy, mistletoe, the sweet-smelling bay and rosemary, and green branches of the box tree. By Candlemas, all had to be gathered up and burnt, or hobgoblins would haunt the house."[33] It was also a symbolic way to let go of the old year and make way for the new.

Along similar lines, a family might have saved a corn dolly representing the Harvest Crone from Lughnassad (also called Lammas, August 2); or made from the last of the harvested grain. If this figure is not going to be recycled as Brigit—the winter crone reborn as the spring maiden—then it should be burned or returned to the fields.

The Brigit's Crosses that have been protecting the house for the past year can be added to the blaze, since you have made new ones to replace them. All this may have been the origin of the spring cleaning tradition, removing the remnants of the past and "clearing the decks" for a busy spring and new year.

Red and White

The colors commonly used to celebrate the holiday are white and red. Many Yule festivals will include a girl or young woman dressed in white with a red sash, and this theme carries over somewhat to Candlemas. One obvious source for these colors, at least in northern Europe, would seem to be white for the snow of the departing winter, and red for the hearthfire or Brigit's eternal flame. It might also be a reminder of the ewes' birthing-blood on the snow as the lambs are born. In some Wiccan traditions white is the color of the Maiden goddess, and red symbolizes the Mother (white for innocence and red for menstrual blood). In ceremonial magick, white stands for purity and red for courage; the Magician in many Tarot decks wears a white robe and red cloak.

Whatever the origin of the custom, it makes for wonderful decorating schemes. White tablecloths and altar cloths are easy to come by, as are red candles. For a little contrast, include early spring flowers. Ritual leaders can wear simple robes of white, with red cords, sashes, or cloaks.

Even the celebratory feast can have a red-and-white theme. White foods such as milk, potatoes, pasta, rice, chicken breasts, pork, white cheeses, and vanilla pudding may be accompanied by red chili, tomatoes, red meats, apples, and strawberries. Some foods have both: cheese with red wax coating, spaghetti with marinara sauce, cherry pie with vanilla ice cream, and even candy canes!

The Sacred Smiths

Brigit was the patroness of smithcraft, in company with Wayland of Britain, Goibniu of Ireland, Hephaestus of Greece, Vulcan of Rome, and, of course, the legendary gnomes who hammered away deep in their mountain halls (and you thought that plume of smoke meant volcanic activity!).

As the hearthfire was the social center of the home, so the smithy was the heart of the village in days gone by. As metal was forged and wrought into useful tools and objects of beauty, and people gathered to watch the smith's magic it became a natural meeting place for the villagers. The young men would play games or engage in contests of skill, the women would meet to discuss community affairs, and a minstrel might entertain with a ballad. Underlying all this activity was an ancient sense of respect, or even reverence, for the arts employed at the forge.[34] An old Irish poem describes the scene:

> *The ringing of its busy bent anvils,*
> *The sound of songs from poets' tongues*
> *The heat of its men at clean contest,*
> *The beauty of its women at high assembly.*
> *Blessings on the Forge!*[35]

Brigit taught the original smiths their art, beginning with how to make and keep the fire. Then she showed them how to shape metal into many forms: plows to till the soil, buckets for milking her cows, weapons to defend the land, and in time, even the nib of the poet's pen and the surgeon's blade.

You need not drag out your anvil and fire up the forge to commemorate Brigit's gift. You know that a horseshoe over your door (with the ends up to hold the luck) will bring good energies to your home;

but leaving it in the fire overnight on Brigit's Eve will make it ever so much more effective. (Be careful taking it out!) Prosperity, protection, good fortune—it's an all-purpose talisman. Tell your horse how lucky he is.

Brigit's Sacred Springs and Wells

Ireland is filled with holy wells. Of the more than three thousand officially list-ed,[36] many are sacred to Brigit either as saint or deity.

In ancient times, pilgrims came to the wells to bring offerings and ask for bless-ings, especially healing. In the centuries before coins were widely used, suppli-cants might toss in rings of brass, silver, or gold. Some would bathe in the sacred waters. Entirely apart from any divine intervention, there may have been healing effects just from the cleansing of skin that rarely encountered a good bath.

Well dressing is still practiced today in several communities. The well is decked with flowers and greens and ribbons, and games and contests are held nearby, as well as the obligatory feast in honor of the saint, goddess, or water sprite resident in the well.

At one town in Cornwall, "Part of the festival involves the dressing of Saint Ea's well with ivy leaves and any early flowers, especially snowdrops, winter-flowering jasmine and even very early daffodils, if any have appeared in Cornwall's balmy

winter weather. . . . The well runs even in very dry summers and has the reputation of healing eye complaints and poor sight, if the water is ritually splashed on them three times."[37]

If you have no sacred wells nearby, recreate the spirit of the event by installing a small fountain in your home or garden. Many tabletop fountains sell for less than $100; and small recirculating pumps cost much less, if you are inclined to build your own pool or fountain. Once you have your fountain in place, invite friends over to help add plantings around it, decorate it, and dedicate it to Brigit. Invite everyone to toss in coins; later gather the money and give it to charity—perhaps one related to healing peoples' vision, such as the Lions' Clubs' projects.

Protection Magick

A protection spell invoking the power of the saint is called "The *Caim* or Sanctuary of Brigit." It is a form of the circle of protection. The same technique might be used with Brigantia when a more active defense is required, or with any other aspect of god or goddess.

To make the *caim*, or "encompassing" as it is also called, stretch out your right hand with the forefinger pointing away from you. Then pivot in place, deosil (clockwise), as you recite the charm. Once created, the protective circle will move with you as you walk and guard you from danger of any kind, physical or spiritual.[38]

The spoken charm below has been adapted by the authors based on similar invocations in the *Carmina Gadelica*, and a piece in the Irish *Saint Broccan's Hymn*.

The Caim of Bride

Be the compassing of Bride around me,
Keeping me from hurt and harm,
Keeping me from wound and woe,
Shielding me from all despair.
The fiery sword of valiant Bride
Defend me from all black swarms.
The shield of blessed Bride

Guard me from all sharp edges.
The cloak of gentle Bride
Encircle and protect me.
This day and every day,
This night and every night,
Be the compassing of Bride about me.

A shorter charm to recite with the caim (and easier to remember if you are nervous or in a hurry), is the following:

O Brigit, spread above my head
Your mantle bright to guard me.[39]

Dancing Back-to-Back

The Imbolg sabbat was sometimes celebrated by an unusual form of folk dance, both in the British Isles and on the Continent. Men and women in pairs would stand back-to-back, link arms, and dance. Whether they were actually able to find a rhythm and do this gracefully is uncertain. However, maybe it was supposed to be awkward: for some it must have been hilarious low comedy, watching couples stagger about and fall over.

Games

The Candle Game

One game popular at Imbolg was simply called the Candle Game. Two or more adults and older children sit in a marked circle on the floor and pass a lit candle around. The rest of the family and friends try to lean in and blow out the candle, without stepping inside the circle. Beware hot wax—a votive candle in a glass holder might work best. Anyone who extinguishes the candle gets a kiss or a treat—perhaps a piece of red-and-white peppermint candy. Stop before anyone gets tired of the game.[40]

Charades

Charades are always fun, and certainly require a good dose of Brigit's inspiration to succeed. If the group is mature enough, you can act out book and movie titles or other modern categories. Or, try pantomiming and guessing words and phrases related to the season (no fair pointing!). Some possibilities:

Smithy	Healer	Red and white
Corn dolly	Candle	Hearth fire
Saint Brigit	Iron	Sheep
Lamb	Anvil	Holy well
Poem	Abbey	Goddess
Girdle	Bride	Brigit's Cross
Ireland	Torchlight	Groundhog
Snowdrift	Crocus	Cow
Milk	Miracle	Beer
Flame	Crown of candles	Mantle

Groundhog Day and Winter Weather

There is a tradition in the British Isles and much of Western Europe that sunny weather on Candlemas day heralds more winter weather to come, but cloudy or stormy weather means that winter has run its course and spring is here to stay.[41] A Scottish couplet says that:

> *If Candlemas Day is bright and clear,*
> *there'll be two winters in the year.*[42]

On the other side of the Atlantic, it's more complicated. Never mind looking at the sky yourself, you must check with a specialist: a groundhog comes forth on the morning of February 2, and if he can see his shadow, we can expect six more weeks of winter.

The groundhog, by the way, has a name—or several names. The best-known in America is Punxsutawney Phil. We can thank Clymer H. Freas for Phil's discovery,

or invention, or at least the name. Mr. Freas was city editor of the Punxsutawney
Spirit newspaper in Pennsylvania in 1887, when he heard of a local group who
hunted and barbequed groundhogs. In an article he named them the Punxsutawney Groundhog Club and declared the Punxsutawney Groundhog to be the
official weather prognosticator.

Today, Punxsutawney Phil lives in a heated hollow log (well, a faux-log replica)
on Gobbler's Knob in Punxsutawney. Each year on February 2, a crowd of local
residents and tourists drag him out of his comfy home and watch to see his reaction to the weather.

All this probably started with the Pennsylvania Dutch legend that spring could
be predicted by the behavior of a hedgehog on February 2. The hedgehog was
transmuted to a woodchuck or groundhog, possibly because the Lenni Lenape
Indians near that area revered *Wojak*—"woodchuck" to the white folks—as an
ancestor of their tribe.[43]

In some Celtic villages, it is not a groundhog that foretells the spring, but the
singing of a lark.[44] This seems infinitely more poetic than the observations of a
rodent; one wonders just how the groundhog got the American franchise for this
sort of activity.

Animals, Plants, and Symbols Sacred to Brigit

Most deities are associated with one or more animals. Brigid seems to have more
than her fair share; of course, she is a multi-talented goddess with great responsi-
bilities, so she can probably use the help![45]

Animals

The Boar: Brigit owned (or at least hosted) the king of the boars, Torc
Triath, which came from the forest to join her swine. The boar was symbol of aggressiveness and battle to the Celts, and was often pictured on
jewelry, weapons, and armor. It is an appropriate companion for Brigit
in her warlike aspect as Brigantia, goddess of martial arts. The Norse

tradition "dictated that pork be eaten on Imbolg, and that the bones be saved as talismans of strength and virility until planting time."[47]

The Cow: A white cow with red ears—the colors are a sign that it was a magickal or fairy cow—provided the milk to nourish young Brigit, when she could not eat the meat of the Druid who raised her. Later she owned a cow whose milk never dried up, and in fact filled a lake three times a day. Brigit as goddess had two oxen named *Fe* (or *Fea*) and *Men* (or *Feimhean*)[46] that raised an outcry when Ireland was threatened.

The Fish: A small spotted fish, species unknown, was said to appear in some of her sacred springs as a harbinger of healing (see p. 50).

The Sheep: Imbolg or Oimelc celebrates the season when sheep are giving birth. It was a very important time to the pastoral Celts, since their flocks and herds were their livelihood and their major form of wealth. It is hardly surprising that Brigit is represented as a kind of "Good Shepherdess." Cirb, king of the wethers (castrated male sheep), is associated with the goddess.

Snake or Serpent: On February 1, a snake was supposed to emerge from its lair, and the following traditional charm was recited:

Early on Bride's morn the serpent shall come from the hole,
I will not molest the serpent nor will the serpent molest me.

This is an odd story for Ireland, which has no indigenous snakes, and never has had any. However, Brigit may be related to all the healing and mother goddesses who were shown with snakes. Moreover, the ancient Celts who grew up in Ireland and never encountered snakes must have considered them to be very magickal creatures, when they heard stories from travelers.

Other Animals: The wolf, bear, and badger have all been mentioned in association with Brigit; the latter two possibly because they were hibernating animals that emerged from their winter sleep at about the time of Imbolg.

The Swan: Sometimes deity manifested as a swan in European mythology, as for example in the legend of Zeus and Leda. Swans mentioned by the Celts would sometimes wear gold or silver chains as an unmistakable sign that they were not ordinary birds, and are linked to Brigit.

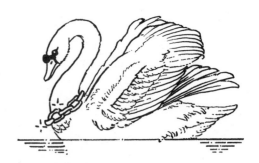

Other Birds: Author Pat Deegan refers to the *Carmina Gaedelica* as including the linnet (*bigein Bride* or "little bird of Bride") and the oyster-catcher (*Bridein* or "Bird of Bride" and *gille Bride* or "page of Bride"). The vulture is occasionally connected with Brigit, which seems strange until you remember her Brigantia aspect as goddess of the battlefield.

Plants

The Blackberry: Next to the oak, this plant is the most closely associated with the goddess Brigit. It represents prosperity and is supposed to be beneficial for stomach complaints, including diarrhea.[48] Have a glass of blackberry wine, a blackberry turnover, or a slice of blackberry pie if you prefer.

Flowers: All the early spring flowers, such as snowdrops, crocuses, and primroses, were naturally associated with the seasonal festivals. "In the county of Shropshire, the snowdrop, first flower of spring, took the place of candles, being named 'Candlemas Bells,' 'Purification flowers' or—with a faint remembrance of Brigit, perhaps—'Fair Maid of February.'"[49] The dandelion also was a favorite of Brigit's: in the *Carmina Gaedelica* it is called *bearnan Bride*, "the little notched [flower] of Bride."

Grain and Hops: Since ale and beer were Brigit's beverages of choice, the plants which provided the raw materials were often special to Her. A mild state of drunkenness was thought to open the mind to inspiration from the goddess; unsurprisingly, poets, bards, and minstrels favored a good malt brew.

The Hazel: The hazel is associated with *cainiu* or keening, invented by the goddess Brigit when she lamented the death of her son Ruadan; and also with satire, an important form of poetry in Celtic society. Nine hazel trees hung over Connlea's Well, a source of magickal inspiration in Celtic mythology.

Herbs: Rosemary, dill, chamomile, and red clover are occasionally mentioned as appropriate herbs for Brigit's Feast Day.[50]

The Oak: The site of Brigit's abbey was *Cill-dara*, the "cell of the oak tree," which gave Kildare its name. Add the story that Brigit was raised by a Druid, or "oak-priest," and it is clear that oaks were sacred to her. They are also associated with the Dagda, the goddess Brigit's father or consort.

Rowan: Luis, or the rowan, is the tree usually assigned to this time of year in the Celtic tree alphabet. It has long been associated with protection, against evil magick as well as disasters such as fire or illness. A sprig of rowan is sometimes put near the door to the home, or over a barn door to keep the animals safe. Rowan berries have a tiny five-pointed star on the bottom, reminiscent of the Witches' protective pentagram.

Willow: Colin and Liz Murray, authors of *The Celtic Tree Oracle*, believe this tree is also sacred to February. The willow symbolizes female energy and the lunar cycle. It has traditionally been used to treat illnesses caused by dampness (and February in Ireland is very damp!). Today, *salicin* is extracted from the bark to treat rheumatism.

Symbols

As a goddess who has her finger in every pie, from poetry to brewing to sovereignty, Brigit has many symbols associated with her.[51]

Brigit's Cross: Her cross was most likely a sun emblem, but may have also represented the four quarters of the year.

The Flame: Fire of all kinds is associated with Brigit, but especially the column of fire seen at her birth, the hearthfire, and the "eternal flame" of Kildare. She is sometimes thought to be a sun goddess as well, and this aspect survives in the solar symbolism of Brigit's Cross.

Iron: It is the metal sacred to her as goddess of smithcraft. Iron plows, horseshoes, tools of all kinds, and weapons are gifts of the skills Brigit bestowed to smiths. Oddly, iron is supposed to be dangerous to fairies, yet Brigit is linked with Faery. Some authors conjecture that the original "fairies" were the short-statured aboriginal peoples of the British Isles, such as the Picts. As a stone-age culture, they were unfamiliar with iron and the frightening weapons made from it. If Brigit or some aspect of her was originally a Pictish goddess, perhaps she was linked with iron by later invaders as a way to claim her for the new tribes and weaken her links with the stone-using peoples.

The Milky Way: As a baby, Brigit was said to have been nourished by the "cosmic cow," which we know today as the Milky Way. Given all Brigit's later connections with cows and with milk, this makes perfect sense.

The Moon: The lunar orb is often connected with the Goddess as Maiden, Mother, and Crone. Brigit is the winter Crone Who transforms into the Maiden of Spring, and the Mother as goddess of fertility. Janet Farrar makes a case for the moon link: "Lunar light is particularly that of inspiration. So it is fitting that Imbolg should be the feast of Brigit, the radiant triple Muse-Goddess. . . ."[53] The image of the moon behind a silhouetted tree has been attributed to her worship.

Nine White Stones: These symbolized the nine virgins attendant on Brigit. They were probably priestesses of the goddess, and later nuns tending the same eternal flame at Kildare. In time their number grew from nine to nineteen.

The Number Eight: Wood reminds us that Brigit is associated with the number eight in the *Book of Lismore*. The author emphasizes that:

On the eighth of the month Brigit was born. . . . in the eighty-eighth (year of her age) she went to heaven. With eight virgins was Brigit consecrated. . . . [Eight] is sometimes said to represent the two spheres, heaven and earth, joined and touching, which is reminiscent of the flame seen to come from the house where the child Brigit was sleeping, which joined heaven and earth. . . ."[52]

The Trinity: The triskelion, or three-armed cross, is often part of Brigit's lore, as is the figure of three concentric circles. This probably referred to her triple nature as the goddess, although later the Church reinterpreted it as the Christian Trinity.

Two Crescents: Two crescents, back to back (like the folk dancers?), symbolized immortality. This symbol was quite popular among the Celtic tribes and appears, for example, on the coinage of Queen Boudicca's Iceni tribe.

Water: This represents both healing and divination, or access to the otherworld of foreknowledge, especially if it comes from a sacred spring or holy well.

Conclusion

There are doubtless a thousand customs related to this season in societies around the world. We can cover only a few of the primary ones associated with Brigit and Imbolg, and there are still more than one individual, family, or group could pack into a single celebration! If you commemorate the holiday annually, you may want to choose a couple of favorite activities that you can enjoy every year, to honor tradition and for continuity; and then vary the rest of your program each time Candlemas comes around.

For example, if your family enjoys making a Brigit dolly and Bride's bed, that custom might become standard every year for you. One year you might also make candles, and another year you could build an outdoor bonfire, or create your own "holy well," with a tabletop fountain, or feast on red and white foods, or hike to a spring, or visit a blacksmith—changing the program every year makes the holiday an adventure!

Remember, though, that every custom, every tradition, and every proverb had a beginning; and you can create your own, as well as borrowing those you like best from history. After all, Brigit is about inspiration—and you honor her and the season when you get creative.

Notes

1. Philomena Rooney of Wexford, quoted in Farrar, *Eight Sabbats for Witches*, p. 63.

2. "Candlemas Customs and Lore," Selena Fox, Circle Sanctuary website.

3. Farrars, *Eight Sabbats for Witches*, p. 66.

4. Pauline Campanelli, *Ancient Ways: Reclaiming Pagan Traditions*, p. 8.

5. Ann Lafferty, "Imbolc," *EarthSpirit* Newsletter, Winter 94.

6. Edain McCoy, *The Sabbats*, p. 94.

7. Campanelli, *Ancient Ways*, p. 8.

8. Ibid., p. 34.

9. Farrars, p. 68.

10. "February 1: Imbolc," Chalice Center website.

11. McCoy, pp. 92–3.

12. Chalice Center website.

13. Alexander Carmichael, *Carmina Gadelica*, IMBAS website.

14. Carmichael, quoted in Chalice Center website.

15. Rhiannon Ryall, *West Country Wicca*, p. 7.

16. Campanelli, *Ancient Ways*, pp. 8–10.

17. Hilaire Wood, in Brigit's Forge website.

18. Campanelli, *Ancient Ways*, p. 14.

19. Liafal, "Brigid: Flame of Two Eternities," ADF website.

20. Lafferty.

21. Chalice Center website.

22. Ibid.

23. Patricia Monaghan, *New Book of Goddesses & Heroines*, p. 69.

24. Liafal, ADF website.

25. Chalice Center website.

26. McCoy, p. 88.

27. Farrars, p. 66.

28. Campanelli, *Ancient Ways*, p. 14.

29. McCoy, p. 89.

30. Farrars, pp. 67–8.

31. Liafal, ADF website.

32. Hilaire Wood, Brigit's Forge website.

33. Doreen Valiente, *An ABC of Witchcraft Past and Present*, p. 359.

34. Brigit's Forge website.

35. NicGrioghair, Branfionn. "Brighid, Bright Goddess of the Gael" via IMBAS website.

36. Farrars, pp. 64–5.

37. Marion Green, *A Calendar of Festivals*, p. 19.

38. Brigit's Forge website.

39. Daughters of the Flame website.

40. Farrars, pp. 66–71.

41. Farrars, p. 66.

42. Chalice Center website.

43. John Shepler, "It's Groundhog Day and the Forecast is . . ." John Shepler's Writing in a Positive Light website.

44. McCoy, p. 92.

45. Selena Fox, "Candlemas Customs & Lore," Circle Sanctuary website. Also Pat Deegan, "Flora and Fauna Associated with Brighid." Shrine website.

46. Chalice Center website.

47. McCoy, p. 98.

48. Ibid.

49. Chalice Center website.

50. McCoy, appendices.

51. "Brigid and Women's Art," source unknown.

52. Brigit's Forge website.

53. Farrars, p. 62.

Divination

Some people want to know the future because they anticipate wonderful things, others because they fear the worst. As winter wanes it is very natural to wonder what lies ahead in the new year; what will blossom in the spring, ripen through the summer, and await our harvest in the fall. Therefore a common part of the Candlemas festival's activities is to perform divination, either as a lighthearted game or a serious magickal undertaking. Ask Brigit's aid; she was seen as the great inspiration behind divination and prophecy, an oracle in her own right.

Here are some techniques you can use; most are ancient, and a few are modern. In all of these, remember that the answers given are trends and probabilities, based on *everything continuing to go the way it is*. If anything changes, the outcome will change. By your choices and actions you direct your future. Divination can only tell you if you are headed in the right direction—or warn you if you are walking into disaster, so you can avoid it.

Pyromancy

Of the many forms of divination available, those having to do with fire, smoke, and candles are the most appropriate for Saint Brigid's Day. Pyromancy means divination using fire, and comes in many forms. Gibson and Gibson list several in their book *Divination and Prophecy*: If a sacrificial fire kindles slowly, it's a bad omen. If it is smoky or crackly, it's still a bad omen. A bright, strong flame burning evenly is the best of signs.[1]

You may not wish to have a sacrificial fire, except possibly to sacrifice marshmallows. The simplest form of pyromancy involves simply staring into the fire. Most of us do this anyway when we sit near a campfire, letting its hypnotic dance lull us into a warm, gentle trance. However, we rarely have a purpose or intent behind our flame-watching, so we are unlikely to receive any messages from the fire.

Pyromancy differs from simple fire-watching in that a specific intent is present, possibly accompanied by a ritual designed to focus the mind to be receptive to any images that may appear. Technically pyromancy is one form of *scrying*, a kind of focused viewing in search of meaningful images, though scryers more often use a crystal ball or magick mirror than flames.

Begin by making sure you can concentrate without distractions. If there are other people in the house, let them know you wish to be undisturbed for a while. Take off your watch—especially if it beeps—and shut off pagers and cell phones. Unplug the regular phone and close the door, and check for anything else that may disturb you. If you have music playing, it should be without words so that all your focus can be on the fire.

Make sure the fire is stoked to the height you want, and make yourself comfortable in front of it. Get a cushion to sit on, or one for your feet if you are in a chair. Roll your neck and shoulders a few times to release tension. Set a notepad and pen beside your hand; you will want to jot down your impressions when it's all over.

Visualize a sphere of light around you as a barrier between you and any distracting energy that may wander into the room. Within your circle you are safe and protected. Ask a favorite deity to watch and protect you, and guide your scrying so that the answers are clear. Formulate your question. It can be as broad as

"What will the coming year hold for me?" or a very specific question about some aspect of your life. Make it short, but remember that yes-or-no questions are not as likely to get a helpful answer as something more open-ended. *"Should I vacation at* Camp Dandelion this year?" is not as helpful as *"What might happen if* I vacation at Camp Dandelion this year?"

Now that you're prepared physically, psychically, and mentally, sit back and focus on the flames while running your question through your mind. Repeating the question to yourself not only helps focus your intent, but also helps keep you from dozing—which is very tempting in front of a cozy fire!

What do you see in the dancing flames? Pictures may appear, but they may vanish just as quickly, so stay focused. They may be people, places, objects—all of the things you are used to seeing in your daily life, and more. The fairies sometimes speak through flames, and the gods and goddesses especially like the activity and life of the fire as a means to communicate.

Listening is also important in pyromancy. The logs may snap and pop, and keep up a merry patter. They may speak to you. And what do you hear from that small voice in your head, the one that is the true voice of the Goddess? Your intuition, the source of your "hunches"?

As the fire burns down to embers, images may appear in the glowing coals. These are frequently easier to read than flames, because the visions tend to last longer. It's also easier to sit before glowing embers without becoming so warmed that you nod off.

When you have received an answer to your question, thank the flames, as well as whatever deity has spoken to you or guided you. Then write down your impressions, even if they seem irrelevant or silly at the moment. Scrying is very much like dreaming, especially lucid dreaming, and answers don't always come in clear, direct form. What you jot down may not make sense right away, but will become clear in a day or a week. Finally, release the circle of protection, get up and stretch, and your pyromancy is finished. Congratulations!

These ritual preparations can be used with any form of divination. Preparing the environment; preparing yourself mentally, physically, and psychically; and writing down the results are standard practice.

More Flame Scrying

Scrying by staring into a candle flame is common, and is similar to staring into a fire. It is not so much the shape of the flame, itself, but what you see in it that gives you a message. Then there is *lampadomancy*, the use of lighted lamps for divination—think of the little oil lamps made of stone or brass, like Aladdin's—in which the appearance and duration of the flames indicate your answers.

Lychnomancy is the use of three lighted candles set in a close triangle, and their flames are interpreted as follows. If they waver back and forth, your circumstances will change. If they twist in spirals, beware of secret plotters. Rising and falling flames mean serious danger. If one flame is brighter, expect good fortune. A sputtering flame indicates disappointment soon. The tip of the wick glowing brightly means increased success, but it will be short-lived if the glow fades. If one candle goes out, there may be a severe loss for someone involved in the reading.

Salt, Bay Leaves, and Dried Peas in the Fire

Using salt for divination is called *alomancy* or *halomancy*. "In Scotland on Imbolg night, it was a tradition for each member of the family to throw protective salt in the fire and divine their immediate futures by the pops and lights it made."[2] This is a subset of *capnomancy*, which covers all forms of "throwing-something-on-the-fire and figuring out what it means."

A specialized version of this is *daphnomancy*, which involves throwing laurel (bay) leaves on the fire. The louder the leaves crackle, the better the omen. Originally, the leaves had to be picked in a grove sacred to Apollo, so we don't know how well it would work today. However, one could always try consecrating a tree in the back yard to the sun god, to see if that works.

In Brittany, "grain sheaves not used to make the Grain Dolly were thrown into the fire. If they were quickly consumed it meant that spring was at hand; if they took a long time to burn, the winter would be a long one. If they broke in half and burned in two distinct pieces, there would be a brief respite from the cold, with more winter to come."[3]

Powdered dried peas, pitch, or almost anything else can be thrown on the fire for divination (but nothing explosive, we trust). Usually the faster something burns, the better the omen. Sudden sparks from knotty logs mean something, as do colored flames from burning driftwood and odd shapes caused by flames or smoke. Your goal is to determine what these omens mean for you. Ask yourself this: when something happens, what is your instant emotional reaction? Trust your feelings. If an event feels scary, if your chest grows tight and your neck tenses up, then it's a warning or negative portent, no matter what any book might say. If your response is a feeling of pleasure or relaxation, it's a good omen. It can be that simple; except that, for many people, tuning in to their own feelings is never simple.

Hearthside Signs of Brigit

Before you leave the hearth, you might try a little *spodomancy*, *tephramancy*, or *tephromancy*: divination by interpreting the ashes of any fire, but particularly a sacrificial fire. When you create "Brigit's Bed" (see chapter 3) near the hearthfire, take some cold ash and lightly sprinkle it in a thin layer on the stone or brick surface before the fire, just before you retire for the night. In the morning, look to see whether there are marks or footprints in the ash. These may look like the fan-shaped prints of a goose or swan, or a mark made by the club that the visiting god carries.

If there are prints, then Brigit herself has visited your home, and her blessings will be with you all throughout the year. If not, an ancient custom decrees that to remedy this, a cock be "buried as an offering at a place where three streams met—a three-fold confluence of sacred power—and incense burned on the fire the next evening."[4] If this is not possible for you, try the modern equivalent: a picnic of fried chicken by any stream, with a campfire to toast marshmallows.

Through the Smoke

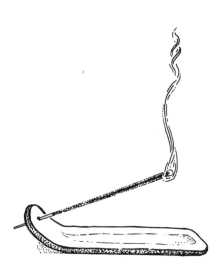

Libanomancy or *livanomancy* is finding meaning in the way the smoke rises from incense. Frequently, the straighter and higher the smoke rises before dissipating, the more positive the omen. Do this away from central-heating air registers, or when the furnace cycles on it will really confuse your divination.

If there are no outside influences that you can detect, but the smoke eddies in an agitated way, that's not good. Occasionally the streamers of smoke may make fascinating shapes such as spirals, and you have a sign that something very significant is about to happen. To determine what it might be, follow up with a more information-rich form of divination.

Water Divination

Pegomancy is particularly appropriate for a celebration of Brigit, because it involves divination by the color and movement of water in springs or fountains. There is very little written on this method, but we can guess at the following correspondences:

- Lots of ripples and eddies mean confusion, conflicting forces at work.

- A swift current means rapid progress.

- A slow, steady current means little change.

- Stagnant water or puddles indicate no progress.

- Clear water indicates good health or that your goals are clear.

- Muddy water indicates illness or fuzzy goals.

Melted Wax in Water

The formal name for this is *ceromancy*, and it is traditionally done by melting wax in a brass bowl and pouring it slowly into another bowl filled with water, then reading the shapes that result. It is the precursor to *tasseomancy*, the reading of tea leaves or coffee grounds.

Formulate your question in your mind, then speak it aloud. Carefully melt some paraffin, wax, or candle stubs in a double boiler. Do *not* melt wax directly over an open flame because the vapors may ignite, causing a dangerous explosion.

Then fill a fairly large pot or cauldron with cold water and slowly pour a little of the liquid wax into it. The wax will harden into a freeform shape as it plunges into the water. Carefully fish it out and place it on a cloth or paper towel. As you study the shape, it may remind you of an animal, plant, or object. Turn the wax and look at it from different angles until it reminds you of something. If necessary, break it into two or more pieces to get simpler shapes. Interpret its meaning for your life by what you see in the shape.

If you are doing this with family or friends, let everyone brainstorm what the shapes look like and what they might mean. Someone might say "It looks like a dolphin . . . that means playfulness to me." Another: "I think it's a shark, and stands for danger!" Another: "I think it's a dolphin, but I think it symbolizes healing." Anyone can make suggestions, but only the one who asked the question decides on the final interpretation, based on their intuition.

We recommend that only adults handle the hot wax, with children of the household keeping well back; the kids can handle the wax shapes when they're cool, and help with the interpretation.

Straw and Hot Iron

Sideromancy is divination by dropping straws (as in hay and straw) onto red-hot iron and interpreting the shapes they take. It's certainly appropriate to a goddess of smithcraft, but probably too hazardous for a family gathering. A group of adults should attempt it only if they have the guidance of a professional metalworker such as a farrier, who can actually heat and handle the iron. We know of no books on the subject to help with interpretation, so as with the melted wax, you would need to rely on brainstorming and intuition.

Bibliomancy

Some Christians use the Bible as a divination tool; you could just as easily use the Chinese **Tao te Ching or I Ching**, the Wiccan "Charge of the Goddess," or any other book that has meaning for you. Because Brigit is a goddess of inspiration and poetry, it seems appropriate on her holy day to ask her for guidance through a poetry book.

Choose any volume of poetry that you enjoy; it can be the collected works of one poet, or a treasury of the works of many famous poets. Think carefully about your question, then open the book "at random" to any page, and without looking, place your finger on the page. Read that line aloud, then copy it out of the book and meditate on it. It may provide some useful answers to your question, or it may point you in another direction that is even more helpful to your situation than the question you originally asked.

A Brigit's Tarot Reading

This works best with a fairly "traditional" deck of Tarot cards, such as the Rider-Waite or Morgan-Greer decks. However, it can be adapted to other decks as well.

First, consider your question carefully. It can be anything, as long as it's not a simple "Yes-No" question, nor a question that invades someone else's privacy. Some examples of things you might ask:

"What would it be best for me to focus on this spring?"

"What kind of job or career would suit me best?"

"What must I do to build a good relationship with _____?" (Insert the name of your girlfriend or boyfriend.)

"What will bring me prosperity in the coming year?"

"How can I insure the best health for myself in the months ahead?"

Shuffle the deck while thinking about your question. Then go through the deck carefully, with the cards face up.

If your question is about an Earth issue such as your job, money, or possessions; or a Fire issue, such as energy, will, or goals; then remove the card that is under (behind) the Eight of Pentacles, which represents Brigit in her aspect as Smith.

If your question is about an Air issue, such as ideas, plans, dreams, or school, then remove the card that is under the Star, which represents Brigit in her aspect as Poet.

If your question is about a Water issue such as emotions, or about your health, then remove the card that is under Temperance, which represents Brigit in her aspect as Healer.

If your question is either more general or more complex, remove all three cards. Study the cards to gain insight to decide what you need to do. Try to look at the card as if you've never seen it before. Ask yourself questions like:

"What was my first impression of the card?"

"What is the figure doing?" or, if there is more than one figure, "What are
    they doing?"

"What is their relationship to each other?"

"What is the figure looking at beyond the card, that I can't see?"

"How does the figure feel about that?"

"What happened just before the figure got here?"

"What are the main colors of the card, and what do they mean?"

"What kind of sound, music, or noise can the figure hear, and what does
    it mean?"

"If I were the figure, what would I do next?" and so on.

Write down your answers and meditate on them. See if you can sum up what
the cards are telling you. If they don't make sense immediately, they will in time;
keep referring back to them until the meaning is clear.

Casting the Stones

Since before the dawn of recorded history, people have been "casting" objects as a
way of understanding their world and their potential future. These can be shells,
bones, twigs, little ceramic tiles with carved runes or other symbols on them, or
stones.

Divination with stones is sometimes called lithomancy. Begin by collecting
some small rocks. These can be stones which have been naturally rounded and
polished by a river or the sea, pretty pebbles you have picked up from the road-
side when out for a walk, or polished semiprecious gemstones purchased at a rock
shop or museum store. This system requires nine stones for a complete set, and
each stone is assigned a meaning and marked with a symbol. The chart below
shows the stones and their symbolism.

To cast them, begin by drawing a circle on the ground, about 12 inches in
diameter. Hold the stones and concentrate on your question; then toss the stones

into the circle. You should drop them from high enough that they spread out over the circle, and a few of them may even bounce outside the line.

Anything that falls outside the circle, you can disregard. The closer a stone is to the center of the circle, the more important it is. Interpret the stones in relationship to each other. For example, the Mars stone near the Jupiter stone could mean that a conflict will expand, or that more assertiveness or action is called for. The Sun stone next to the Venus stone could mean success in love. Earth and Saturn stones in close proximity may mean limited prosperity; Earth with the Jupiter and Sun stones means increased prosperity, or that a project relating to your home will go very well. Find the interpretation that best fits the wording of your original question.

Lithomancy Stones

Stone	Meaning	Gemstones	Symbol
Earth Stone	Home, prosperity, or material possessions	Any jasper, petrified wood, or fossil	⊕
Moon Stone	Magick, intuition, or emotions	Moonstone or angel agate	☽
Sun Stone	Success or healing	Sunstone, tiger's eye, or citrine	☉
Mercury Stone	Communications or travel	Clear quartz or any agate	☿
Venus Stone	Love or relationships	Green aventurine or rose quartz	♀
Mars Stone	Action, assertiveness, or conflict	Red jasper or bloodstone	♂
Jupiter Stone	Expansion or education	Amethyst or sugilite	♃
Saturn Stone	Limitation or obstacles	Obsidian, black onyx, or Apache Tear	♄
"X" Stone	An unknown factor, not yet predictable	Anything unusual: holy stone, tektite . . . ?	X or ?

As with any system, remember that the stones can only show you trends and probabilities. Nothing that lithomancy shows you is carved in stone. By your choices and actions you direct your future. Divination can only tell you if you are headed in the right direction—or warn you if you are not.

Dreaming

Like most artists, many poets get great inspiration from their dreams. Brigit was probably no exception.

Some people remember their dreams often and in great detail; for others, dreams are elusive and vanish like a morning mist the moment they awaken. Some dreams are prophetic, and those are the ones we wish we could remember. However, we don't know before sleeping (and sometimes not when we wake!) which ones will be prophetic. In order to catch any prophetic dreams, you must train yourself to remember all your dreams. You can then write them down and learn to interpret them for yourself.

The interpretation of dreams is a little more challenging, and very personal. Only you can tell what that green elephant going over a waterfall in a rubber raft means. Dream interpretation books may be helpful if you're really stuck, but they are often based on cultural symbols and stereotypes that may not apply to you. The best bet is to keep a dream journal for several months, then go back and read the entries to find common threads or symbols.

By paying attention to your dream diary and correlating what happens in your waking life, you may find out that the elephant dream appears about a week before every exam, and that you do well when he is in a rubber raft, but not when he's on a bicycle. Then perhaps you can study a little harder when he appears on the bicycle! As we've said before, divination is merely an indication of what will happen if things continue on as they are going. By deciding to study the Thursday before your exam instead of going to the party as you had planned, you are changing the course of events.

Conclusion

There are a thousand other forms of divination that we have not mentioned. The ancient Chinese sometimes heated the shoulder bone of an ox, and read the future from the cracks. Others would observe the shapes of clouds, the flight of an arrow, or the layers in an onion. But in the end it is not the tool or method that matters. Divination is about receptive consciousness opening to the hidden understanding of your deep mind; and it is about trusting your instincts. When you can simultaneously open and focus your mind, allow images to appear, and pay attention to your intuition as you interpret them, you will know how to divine your future—your shifting, mutable, possible future as it appears at that moment.

People have always looked for portents in the skies, the flames of their fires, or on the face of a Tarot card. As long as you remember that your life is yours to create and guide, divination can be fun and useful. Candlemas is a perfect time to perform divination about the coming warm months, and we hope you have enjoyed this selection of divination methods to bring the wisdom of Brigit to your plans for your future.

Notes

1. All definitions not otherwise attributed are from Gibson and Gibson, *The Complete Illustrated Book of Divination and Prophecy,* pp. 311–325.

2. McCoy, *The Sabbats,* p. 101.

3. Ibid. p. 102–103.

4. Chalice Center website.

Cleansing and Purification

Once upon a time, when people bathed once a year and the rushes had been strewn in September and were getting rank by February, spring cleaning was a very serious business. The rushes, and all their tiny inhabitants, were swept out the door, the one or two sets of clothes were washed, and the annual bath was endured. Doreen Valiente says in *An ABC of Witchcraft Past and Present*: "By Candlemas . . . a new tide of life had started to flow through the whole world of nature, and people had to get rid of the past and look to the future. Spring cleaning was originally a nature ritual."[1]

So what is spring cleaning today?

Most of us live in a society where a primary emphasis is on acquiring goods and money. We are encouraged to want more of everything: more food, more clothes, bigger houses, fancier cars, more electronic gadgets. However, many spiritual seekers would be quick to say that there is an imbalance in this constant striving for wealth and possessions. Spiritual people are notable not only for what they have, but also for what they choose not to include in their lives. Some of the greatest spiritual teachers have had simple or even ascetic lifestyles. Free from the need to acquire, maintain, repair, protect, handle, and store stuff, they were able to focus on the great essentials: harmony with the divine, and with the community of living beings.

This is not to say that we must all live in poverty with only a breechcloth and rice bowl to our names, in order to grow spiritually. However, an obsession with things can definitely impede progress. The first question is, how much stuff is enough, and how much is too much? The second question is, do we use our possessions, or do they use us?

There would seem to be a spiritual necessity for occasional cleansing and releasing—the universe is not simply Maiden energy, which is expansive, and Mother energy, which is nurturing, but also the Crone energy which removes, releases, ends, and destroys. The Hindus would say that a world without Kali and Shiva, the Destroyers, would be horribly out of balance.

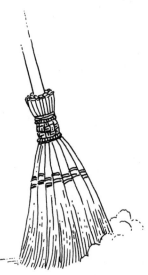

Cleansing and purification are two aspects of this necessary process; they are ways to release what is unnecessary or harmful. This might include the trash in your garage, the clutter in your house, the toxins in your body, the fears in your heart, or the falsehoods in your mind. Getting rid of all this leaves room for new, fresh, and healthy things to come into your life . . . or simply gives you space in which to breathe and be.

With spring approaching, get ready for the new season by cleansing your life—your body (inside and out), your mind and heart, your home, and your religious places and tools. Let's work from the inside out.

A Cleansing Fast

Intelligent fasting can leave you feeling clear and energized. Of course, always check with your physician or health-care professional before you make any drastic changes in your lifestyle, especially if you have any chronic health conditions. Ask about the following kinds of fast:

- Liquid fast—Avoid solid foods, but make sure you stay hydrated with water, clear soups, fruit and vegetable juices, and healthful herb teas.

- Fruit fast—You can live well on fruits for a while, but they tend to clean out the intestines quickly, so approach this fast carefully. Stock up on varied organic fruits: bananas, apples, berries, melons, and tomatoes.

- Vegetarian fast—If you normally eat meat, especially red meat, you can give your insides a welcome change of pace by going strictly vegetarian for a few days. But do not replace meat with sugary, salty junk foods. Plan ahead to eat whole-grain breads, cereals, and pastas; a variety of green and yellow vegetables lightly steamed; some salad, and fresh fruit. Go easy on dairy products.

Generally a fast should accomplish its purpose in one to three days. Come off the fast gradually—don't stuff yourself with all your favorite heavy foods the minute it's officially over! And when you slowly resume your regular diet, maybe you can take advantage of the transition by making one or two healthful changes, such as replacing black tea with green tea, or refined sugar with honey. Brigit the Healer would approve!

A Ritual Bath

Are you a person who grabs a quick shower before you fling on your clothes and rush off to work? Then it's time to make bathing an event to remember. Here are the ingredients:

- A bathtub filled with very warm, not-quite-hot water, preferably scented with bath oils or an infusion of herbs; bubbles are recommended but optional.

- Gentle light provided by several candles or votive lights scattered about the room.

- Soft music; your choice of classical (Bach? Vivaldi?), instrumental meditation music (Kitaro? Clannad?), or spiritual chants and songs (Goddess-oriented choirs? Gregorian chants?).

- Some words reflecting your spiritual tradition: praying aloud, repeating an affirmation or mantra, reading the Charge of the Goddess or other inspiring literature.

You will want to soak a long time, and then vigorously wash every inch of you from hair to toenails.

Lest we sound "indoorsist," we should remind you that there may be ways to have a ritual bath *outdoors*. Are you the proud owner of a hot tub, or do you have a generous friend with one? Or do you live in an area with natural warm springs or hot springs accessible to the public? One of Amber's fondest memories is the Christmas eve she spent in a hot spring high in the mountains, looking out over a spectacular vista of endless peaks disappearing in the fading twilight, and soaking in the warm water by candlelight as snowflakes drifted out of the dark winter sky.

Releasing Negative Emotions

Are you a person who expresses your deepest feelings easily and often? Do you laugh a lot and then cry at the drop of a romantic movie? Or are you Mr. or Ms. Self-Control, always outwardly calm and disciplined? If the latter sounds like you, you may need to cough up some of those emotional hairballs you've been hoarding inside. Emotional catharsis can leave you feeling lighter, happier, more alive to the world around you, and even more loving and intimate with the people closest to you.

There are many ways to open up emotionally. For some, all it takes is a quiet, private space, a sympathetic ear to listen—and a shoulder to cry on. For others, counseling may be needed to overcome habitual barriers—either with a professional therapist or your priest, priestess, or minister.

Or take a long walk by yourself in nature, and tell your deepest griefs and greatest joys to Goddess or God, along the seashore, deep in the forest, or high in the mountains. To jump-start, you can recall and describe the moments in your life that have affected you most deeply—the hurts and losses not yet healed, the times when you triumphed over adversity, or simply the times you knew you were loved. A note of caution and common sense: if you are depressive, bipolar, or have thoughts of suicide, do this kind of work only with a professional counselor.

A Mental Clearing Exercise

To paraphrase an inspirational poster, "trust thy body all the days of thy life, for thy mind doth mess with thee." It is true that our splendid human brains can be wonderful tools, but they can also be our worst enemies. Almost everyone knows what it's like to realize suddenly that we have been believing information that's inaccurate, or holding on to a negative attitude that does us more harm than good, or harboring an idea that's just plain dumb. Ouch! Time to do a spring cleaning upstairs in your head.

Now, brainwashing or a prefrontal lobotomy might do the trick, but we recommend gentler methods. One approach is to write down all your values, principles, and key beliefs as to how the world works. Discuss them with wise friends, spiritual leaders, or counselors, and then take a good, hard, honest look at them. Are they supported by the facts? Do they make the world a better place when you act on them? And do they *work* for you—i.e., make you a happy, productive person?

Examining your mental foundations alone is no easy task, which is why you want other people whose judgment you trust to be part of the process. They cannot tell you what to believe, but they can ask you tough questions and make sure you don't avoid facing hard truths.

What happens if you discover some mental baggage that you want to get rid of? We suggest a two-part process. First, hold a ritual to release the old stuff. Write down that wrong information, those half-truths, those damaging beliefs. Then tie the paper to a helium balloon and—Bon Voyage! Or put it under a rock in a fast stream. Or bury it someplace you won't be able to find again. Or burn it in a cauldron. Or mail it to a fictitious city—and don't include your return address.

Then write down and reaffirm your new beliefs. Nature abhors a vacuum—so be really clear as to what you're replacing the erroneous stuff with, or you might slip back into your old ways of thinking. You can summarize your new thinking in an affirmation, tape copies to your bathroom mirror and other spots around your home and office, and repeat it several times a day. Embroider it on a sampler; send it to yourself in a telegram; put it on the bottom of every e-mail you send out; translate it into Latin and put it on your family coat-of-arms; bake a cake, write it in frosting, and devour it.

An Elemental Self-Cleansing

Symbolically cleanse the area with either salt water or burning incense. Cast the circle. (If you don't know how, then simply imagine a ring of blue fire around you, expanding into a sphere of energy, which keeps out anything negative and holds in everything positive.) Invite the powers of Air, Fire, Water, and Earth to lend their energies to your work. Now visualize your favorite image of Deity appearing in the circle and speaking to you, explaining that you have a good heart and strong spirit, and are about to be cleansed of anything that tarnishes or weakens them.

Now take up the incense (a sage smudge stick works well for this), and waft the smoke all over you, saying: "By the Four Winds and the powers of mind, intellect, and imagination, I am cleansed." Imagine a clean, crisp, cool breeze blowing through every cell of your body.

Then take up a candle (some people prefer a large, red candle), and quickly pass your hand through the flame, saying: "By the Flames of Hearth and Sun, and the powers of energy, will, and passion, I am cleansed." Imagine a wildfire roaring through you, burning away all pollution and impurity but leaving you unharmed.

Next, take up a chalice of pure water (a silver one would be lovely, but any material will do), sip the water, then sprinkle some on your face, saying: "By the Seven Seas and the powers of love, emotion, and intuition, I am cleansed." Imagine swimming through the whitewater of an icy mountain river.

Take up the bowl of salt, and sprinkle a little on yourself, saying: "By the Body of our Mother Earth, and the powers of health, prosperity, and the physical realm, I am cleansed." Imagine lying in a field of grain, or on the flank of a mountain, and letting all that is negative or unclean flow out of you, to soak into the earth and be transformed.

Lastly, take up a vial of sacred oil (or your favorite cologne will do), and touch a drop to your forehead, saying: "By the Divine Spirit in all things, and the powers of love, wisdom, and strength, I am cleansed." Imagine the Deity reaching out to touch you, and suffusing your entire being with a pure, white radiance. With it comes an incredible sense of purity, lightness, and joy.

Sit quietly for a moment and reflect on ways that you can "act in accord" by living a cleaner and more wholesome lifestyle. Then dismiss the Elements, thank the Deity you invited, and open the circle.

A Self-Blessing Ceremony

A self-blessing ritual is a natural follow-up to personal purification. This is an excellent thing to do just before retiring for the night; your deep mind will have a chance to absorb the message while you sleep. Here's our favorite version, step by step:

1. Take a ritual bath and dress in a clean, simple white robe (or go skyclad; that is, wearing only the sky).

2. Ground and center.

3. Asperge (ritually cleanse the area, either with incense, salt and water, or both).

4. Cast the circle (see p. 110).

5. Call the Quarters (invite the Elements of Air, Fire, Water, and Earth).

6. Invite your favorite deities.

7. Take up a silver chalice of mixed water and white wine, or simply water with a touch of salt in it, and proceed as follows:

   a. Dip your fingers in the wine mixture, touch your feet, and say aloud: "Blessed be my feet which have brought me in these ways."

   b. Touch your genital area and say: "Blessed be my loins, which bring forth life and pleasure."

   c. Touch your heart, and say: "Blessed be my breast, formed in beauty and in strength."

   d. Touch your lips, and say: "Blessed be my lips, which shall speak the Names of the Goddess and the God."

   e. Touch your eyes, and say: "Blessed be my eyes, which see Thy beauty all around me."

f. Touch your forehead, and say: "Blessed be my self, child and heir of all that is holy."

8. Sit quietly and meditate on a picture of yourself, or gaze at yourself in a mirror, remembering that you are loved and worthy of love. (Mirror-gazing can be emotionally difficult the first few times; have a box of tissues handy and allow yourself to cry if you need to.)

9. Thank your deities and bid farewell to the Quarters. Open the circle.

10. Rest.

11. Repeat at least once a week until you truly believe you are loved, then continue once a month.

Out with the Old Stuff

Has your home become filled with clutter that you never use but might need someday? Clutter slows you down, and blocks the achievement of your desires. You especially do *not* need useless clutter at the beginning of a fresh new year, when all your splendid goals, dreams, and aspirations are beckoning!

We can hear you saying, "Yes, but. . . ." Yes, you've tried a hundred times to clean out all that stuff, and it's still there. Well, here are some tips that can help you make it happen. If you are a packrat, take your courage in both hands and follow these suggestions.

- Don't try it alone. Let us guess—you don't want other people sorting your stuff—what if they throw out something important? (The recipe for Chutney Corn Bread, the 1983 letter from Aunt Mabel asking for the name of that book, the broken but beloved toy from your childhood—the electric bill from three houses ago?) Sorry, invite trusted friends anyway; they can be a great help. If you need to, set rules such as "You can organize, but don't throw anything away until you check with me."

- Assign a place for everything—no miscellaneous piles waiting for a home.

- Add storage space if you must. Friends can put up shelves, convert an unused bedroom or attic to a storage area, build a loft, bring in a filing cabinet, and so on. Maybe it's time to buy or build an outdoor storage shed—have a "barn-raising" with your friends. Even an 8 by 10-foot shed can hold an enormous amount.

- Rent a storage space. This is a tremendous incentive to actually get rid of stuff. After all, a typical storage space costs $50 per month or more. Don't you have something better on which to spend $600 per year than storing stuff you never use?

- Consider removing furniture that's not used, to give you more floor and wall space. Sometimes furniture can double as storage—such as a window seat with a lid, or a platform (with drawers) for a futon.

- Want to get radical? On a nice sunny day, clear *everything* out of a given room and put it on your lawn. Then clean the room, thoroughly, and start putting the items back (or dumping or donating them) one at a time in an organized way. With some help, you could do one room per weekend and do the whole house once-over in just a few weeks—unless you live in the Hearst Mansion or Buckingham Palace.

- Hold a garage sale and give the money to some worthy cause.

- Most importantly, establish *systems* for dealing with things. This will include habits such as tossing out junk mail unopened, taking newspapers and bottles to the recycling center every Saturday morning, or making a rule that each time you buy one new item for your home, two must go into a garage sale or charity donation box.

Spring House Cleaning

Spring-cleaning is ever so much easier if you do it in concert with an anti-clutter campaign. The basic rule is that every surface gets cleaned; for a little magickal boost, put some rosemary or another blessing herb in the wash water. It is important to approach this cleaning not as a tiresome chore, but as a gift to yourself and the goddesses of hearth and home. Play music, work with friends, pause and appreciate the work you've done every so often, and finish each day with a bath and a wonderful supper. Follow the physical house cleaning with a spiritual House Cleansing and Blessing Ritual.

House Cleansing and Blessing Ceremony

Once your home is clean and uncluttered, you may want to spiritually cleanse and bless it . . . especially if any of the following apply:

- The house has not been purified since you moved in;

- There has been serious illness in the home since your last house blessing;

- There have been arguments or even physical violence in the house;

- Anyone in the house has been very depressed or unhappy for any reason; or

- If any hardship or tragedy has befallen the residents.

There are many "recipes" for a ceremony like this, but we will share our favorite:

1. Gather family and friends; have them bring food for a potluck later, and house gifts if they wish.

2. Obtain the following materials: bells, gongs, and rattles, or pots, pans, and wooden spoons; light blue candles for purification; pure water in a bowl; salt; sage incense bundles or sticks; light pink or rose candles for blessing; rosemary oil; and two pieces of rose quartz for each door to the outside.

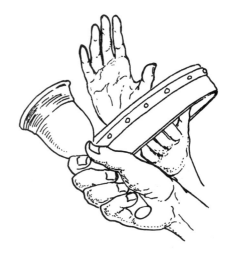

3. Bring everyone to the heart of the house; it might be the kitchen table, the living room, your bedroom, or someplace else. You will know where it is; it's the place where you feel most comfy, and probably spend most of your time. Sit in a circle, hold hands, and attune to one another. Imagine the house glowing with a clear light, filled with love and happiness. Then hum or chant, imagining the sound waves moving out in expanding circles and washing all negative energies from the house.

4. Process through the house, starting at the front door and moving widdershins (counterclockwise). Take the noisemakers with you, and make a terrible racket, clanging, banging, ringing and drumming. Yell things like "Gloom, begone!" or "Illness, leave this house!"

5. Process through again, widdershins. This time let people smudge every door, window, vent, and corner with the sage sticks; and sprinkle them with salt water. You may wish to say "I cleanse you with Fire and Air; I cleanse you with Earth and Water." Extra people can carry the blue candles.

6. Once more go through the house, this time moving deosil (sunwise, clockwise). As you process, sing a chant such as:

> *Goddess, Spirits, bless this place,*
> *Love and joy fill each space;*
> *Front to back and side to side,*
> *Health and wealth and safety bide.*

Let one person anoint each windowsill, doorsill, and opening by drawing a small pentagram with the rosemary oil. This blesses and seals the home. Another person should place a rose quartz stone on each side of every door to the outside, to allow only positive energy into the house. (If you have small children who might swallow the stones, fix them firmly at the top of the sills out of reach, or use 2-inch-diameter stones that can't be swallowed.) Additional friends can carry the pink candles.

7. Gather again at the heart of the house, and hold hands while someone speaks a benediction, such as "May all who dwell within or enter this home, live in love and laughter always. Blessed be." Then play some music, break out the food, and party!

Spring Yard Cleaning and Landscaping

As long as you're cleansing the inside of your house, you may as well do the outside—assuming you have an outside, and are not living in Apartment #5073 in a high-rise in the middle of Manhattan.

If you do have a yard, even a little one, clean it up. Pick up trash, water the plants, seed any bare spots, and clip the bushes. If need be, paint the exterior of your house, or at least those peeling spots on the trim. Then think, "landscaping." Is there room for an herb garden? A rock garden? A trellis with ivy or rose bushes? A birdhouse? A little shrine to your favorite deity? A recycling fountain? A nine-hole golf course? Well, maybe not a nine-hole golf course. Still, you can undoubtedly find a way to add beauty to your outdoor space. Ask Brigit for inspiration.

Creating a Sanctuary Room

You may have the luxury of having enough rooms in your house that you can dedicate one to be a personal temple or sanctuary, and nothing else. This is a quiet, simple room that exists only as a place of peace, rest, relaxation, meditation, and re-creation. You might use this room for personal ritual, yoga, or tai chi, or the occasional Tarot reading. Some suggestions:

- Clean out the room thoroughly, and if the walls need painting, choose a light, relaxing color—possibly ivory or pale rose.

- Then put very little back into it. Space and simplicity should characterize the room.

- What little you do put in should be aesthetically pleasing. A personal altar? A single vase of fresh flowers? One or two works of art? A tiny fountain? What objects help bring you to peace and harmony?

- Keep it clean and uncluttered. Each time you use the room, clean up after yourself immediately.

It is very pleasant knowing that, however messy and busy the rest of the house becomes, there is always one room that is an oasis of peace and simplicity.

(Re)Creating Your Personal Altar

Properly used and maintained, a personal altar can be the visible and tangible focus of your spiritual work—a powerful and attractive tool that reminds you who you are at the core of your being. Perhaps you already have an altar in your home, and regularly pray or meditate or perform magick before it. Perhaps you change the altar cloth color and furnishings often, to reflect the changing seasons or your personal spiritual needs.

Or . . . perhaps you have an altar but haven't touched it in months. Is the dust getting a little thick? Have the spiders even abandoned their cobwebs to search for a fresher homesite? It's definitely time to renew or recreate the altar.

And perhaps you have never had a home altar. Well, this is a great time of year to begin. Find or make a flat surface that will be safe from kids and pets. You can make or buy a small table; some people prefer a round top, others like a square one. The material can be anything from polished wood to a slab of stone; but if the surface is not attractive, cover it with an altar cloth. You could also use a dresser top or even one shelf in a bookcase.

The traditional accouterments for a magickal altar include two candles or "lamps of art"; various objects to symbolize Earth, Air, Fire, and Water; and a picture or statue of your favorite Deity (many people include both Goddess- and God-images). You may also keep some of your ritual tools on the altar, such as an athame, wand, and Tarot deck.

For an altar dedicated to Brigit, include an image of her, perhaps as the Lady with the crown of candles. Add a large red candle, or perhaps a red glass votive holder for Fire, since she is a fire goddess. Obtain symbols of her three aspects as Healer, Smith, and Poet—perhaps a bunch of dried healing herbs, tied with a red ribbon; a tiny anvil or craft tool, or something you have made with your hands; and a handwritten or calligraphied poem.

With a red altar cloth use white candles, and vice versa. Add incense or a feather for Air; a chalice or shell for Water; and a bowl of salt, a pentacle, or a favorite stone for Earth. Consecrate the altar to Brigit with appropriate words, such as:

> *Holy Brigit, Triple Goddess, You Who are Healer, Smith, and*
> *Poet, I welcome You. I have created this altar in Your honor, and*
> *in the hope that Your essence will dwell here to heal, re-create,*
> *and inspire me. Lady of Flame, Light of Hope and Life, bless*
> *me, bless this altar, and blessed be your eternal fire.*

Cleansing and (Re)Consecrating Your Ritual Tools

If you have any magickal or religious tools or objects in your home, now is the time to clean them. Polish silver, brass, and copper; rub a little tung oil or lemon oil on the wood; wash the altar cloths; remove the wax drippings left by candles; scrub out the cauldron; and so on.

Once cleaned, purify them in salt or salt water, or sunlight, if the tool will be harmed by salt. If you have not consecrated your ritual tools or religious jewelry, do that next. Within a cast circle, or at least a ceremonial atmosphere (incense, candles, and music), you will need to name yourself, state the purpose of each object, offer it in service to the appropriate deity, and ask Her or His blessing on it. This may be done individually, at an initiation, or in a group ritual. For example:

> *Sweet Aphrodite, Goddess of Love and Lady of the Sea, I am*
> *Laurel, and I come before You as your daughter and priestess. I*
> *place before You my new silver chalice, which symbolizes the*
> *mystery of Your womb, and will be used for divination and to*
> *share the sacred wine within our circle. I offer this chalice in*
> *Your service; may it be used only with love and wisdom, and*
> *may Your blessing be upon it from this day forward. So mote*
> *it be!*

Or:

> *Herne, Great Hunter, Horned One, I call*
> *upon You. I am Will Oakworthy, and I am*
> *here to ask Your blessing. Here is my staff*
> *of magick, which I have carved from oak*
> *and decorated with feathers and polished*
> *stones. It has been created to direct energy*
> *and be my companion in the woods, to sup-*
> *port and help me. I offer this staff in Your*
> *service; may it be used only for good, and*
> *with harm toward none. Please bless it and*
> *fill it with Your strength. Blessed be.*

When you have cleaned and consecrated your tools, wrap them in a clean cloth and lay them away until your next ritual.

A Workplace Clearing Ceremony

Many of us have offices or workplaces that could use some psychic cleansing. Remember how Fred spent a whole week grumbling when the payroll computer burped and he got a check in the amount of 43 cents? Or the time that Martha overheard Ralph's comment about her toy poodle and let him have it with both barrels? All that negative energy (as well as the positive stuff) tends to linger—why not "clean house" at work?

Start by cleaning your work area on the physical plane. Maybe you can get the custodian to do part of it, but if necessary do it yourself. Sweep, vacuum, and wash. Remove clutter: sort, file, and discard. Air out the place if necessary.

The next step is harder. If you come to work in ritual robes with drums and incense, and sprinkle everything with salt water and rose petals, you will get odd looks or maybe a free visit to the company shrink. Subtlety is called for. If you have a private area, sit quietly there, ground and center. Then inhale deeply, draw energy from the Earth or Sun, and as you exhale send it flowing out in concentric circles. Visualize it as light that sweeps all negative energies before it, and completely out of the area. Do this for several minutes. If you can do so without attracting attention, hum as you exhale.

Visualize a circular boundary around the workplace, a wall of blue light or flame that will allow positive energies in but block anything negative. If you wish, anchor the boundary in a large quartz crystal or chunk of rose quartz, placed where it won't attract attention.

Then make a list of all the good things that have happened at work, to remind you that there is more to your job than the upsets and problems. Act in accord by planning some action that will bring more positive energy in: compliment a fellow employee, bring home-made cookies to share during break, do an unexpected favor that will make somebody's work a little easier.

Do all this on a fairly frequent basis, and your workplace will feel markedly better.

Conclusion

Most of us bathe our bodies often and brush our teeth; we like to think of ourselves as having the habit of cleanliness. Doesn't it make sense to extend this way of life to our homes, hearts, minds, and spirits? By doing this cleansing and purification at Imbolc, you will be ready to face your warm-weather activities with a fresh outlook and peace in your heart.

Notes

1. Valiente, ABC of Witchcraft, pp. 65–66.

Celebrations
and Rituals

No matter whether you are celebrating Candlemas by yourself or in a group, your celebration will be enhanced with decorations and music. Here are some suggestions for setting the stage.

The Setting

Decorations for Imbolg or Candlemas should reflect the themes of the season. Gold or brass is always appropriate, as are red and white. Evergreen boughs can represent Brigit's green mantle and the departing winter, and pussy willows, crocuses, snowdrops, and hazel catkins can symbolize the coming of spring.

Celtic knotwork is appropriate, and any of the art books by George or Ian Bain or Courtney Davis can show you Celtic designs appropriate to the season. Brigit's crosses (see chapter 3) can be used in abundance. Remember that Brigit was known for all the holy wells and springs dedicated to her, so a small tabletop fountain as discussed earlier would be a charming addition. If possible set it in a nest of evergreen boughs with early-blooming flowers like crocus and hyacinth adding delightful touches of color.

Place a wreath of boughs and flowers holding several candles on the table as a centerpiece for the feast. See chapter 7 for ideas for candles you can make yourself. (If candle-making is not going to be the main activity of your celebration, consider having a candle-making party the weekend before, so you have lots of homemade candles for the celebration.) In the middle of the wreath you could honor the Poet, Smith, and Healer by placing a favorite book of poetry, a small anvil, and a few bunches of dried healing herbs.

Brigit has a close relationship with the world of Faery, so scatter a few small fairy decorations among the silver, gold, and pastel glitter. Brigit's sacred animals include sheep, cows, bears, pigs, geese, and swans, so a few animal figurines may find places among the evergreens and spring flowers.

Decorating your bed can be a whole delight in itself. If you have the funds and the storage space, consider buying a set of white flannel sheets and a bright red comforter to use every year at Imbolg. If you have four-posters, hang them with swaths of dark green fabric, tied with big red bows and white lace ribbons. Perfume the bedroom with bayberry or cinnamon candles. (Be sure to blow out the candles before you go to sleep!)

Any table can be covered with a white flannel sheet and sprinkled with silver glitter, to symbolize the snows of winter, with early spring flowers as a counterpoint. Be lavish with the use of red fabric and gold glitter, to signify the Sun and the solar theme of the holiday. Fire and ice are always nice.

Incenses appropriate to the season include the single-wood incenses, like cedar, pine, and juniper, as well as blends special to the season that you can make yourself. Scott Cunningham has some wonderful ideas and recipes in *The Magic of Incense, Oils & Brews*.

If you are doing ritual in someone's living room, cover the TV, computer, and stereo with brightly-colored fabric. Always turn off the phones (both landline and cell) and pagers, and take off watches, especially beeping ones. If there's a fireplace, light a good fire about an hour before the ritual starts, and put a large log on just as you begin. That way you won't have to tend the fire in the middle of your activities.

The Altar

The Brigit altar might be covered with a white cloth, symbolizing the white mantle of snow outside. Add a green swath of fabric for Brigit's green cloak, and red candles in candleholders of brass, to symbolize the ascendancy of the sun. A small anvil, a book of poetry, and a bunch of dried herbs honor the Smith, Poet, and Healer. Place on the altar symbols of any illnesses or injuries you have recovered from during the last year, as thanks, or as symbols of those situations you want Lady Brede's help with during the coming year. Very few of us are smiths, but we do have creative projects we are working on, so perhaps place a symbol of one of those on the altar.

It's fun and educational to create four Quarter altars. In the east honor Poetry, using your favorite poetry, art, and calligraphy, on a cloth of deep gold or light blue. For the south, Smithcraft, use a small anvil (see the appendix for a source), a small hammer, your athame, and a red candle or a cotton-ball-and-alcohol fire in a small cauldron, all placed on a red or red-and-gold cloth. In the west, for healing, place your tabletop fountain on a light blue or light green drape, along with dried herbs and a few bottles of tinctures or pots of salve you made the previous summer. And in the north, on a purple drape for sovereignty, place a sword or scepter and crown (or pictures of them), plus a scroll to signify the Law.

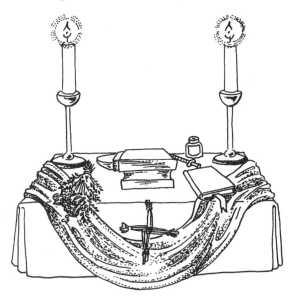

The Music

The music of Brigit's time has mostly been lost, and what survives is primarily Christian ecclesiastical. However, in recent years Celtic music has enjoyed a great revival, and we think Brigit would be happy to be celebrated with Irish harp and bodhran (the Celtic drum). If you don't play yourself, put a CD into the boom box and enjoy. You can use this as background music through the whole celebration, save one piece for a lively dance, or just have music at the beginning and during the feast afterward.

Rituals

Imagine yourself in a small village, where everyone is related. The winter has been long and cold, but the light has begun to return, and the lambs are being born. It is time to celebrate the first hint of spring with a blessing for the home and our work in the year to come:

> If any were found, the first shy snowdrops or early violets, or later, bright golden or purple crocuses, were placed about the house, alongside swathes of dark green ivy leaves. Each of the women poured a libation of milk or water with honey in it and made a wish. Later on, the menfolk were summoned, ribbons or greenery were wound about their heads and arms, and after they had paid a small fee, a coin, a flower posy or even a kiss to the Lady of the house, they too could enter the circle of firelight and ask for help with their work, the craft or trade they would be following throughout the coming year.[1]

You can celebrate the themes of the season by yourself, with your family, among a small group of friends, or in a community gathering. The rituals outlined here were designed by Wiccan priests and priestesses for a primarily Pagan readership. If you are of another faith, feel free to borrow any of the ideas and activities and adapt them to your own beliefs. This holiday is for anyone who wants to enjoy it!

A Candlemas Rite for One

This is a wonderful ritual to do on the evening of February 1, just before you go to bed. It can easily be adapted for a group, though the ritual baths would have to be done at participants' homes before they gather—unless you have a big hot tub!

Begin by cleaning your bathroom. Gather votive candles, music, incense, and whatever you like to put in the water: bubble bath, herbs in muslin bags, bath oils, etc. Lay out a clean robe and whatever jewelry you prefer to wear for ritual. Then thoroughly clean the room where you plan to hold your ritual.

Set up the altar. You will need the following:

An altar cloth of red, white, or both these colors

Five unlit candles, preferably white or red, and matches

A bowl of water and small container of salt

Incense and a burner

A chalice, cup, or goblet, filled with pure water or a healing herbal tea
   such as chamomile

A picture or symbol of something you have created, or the thing itself

A small stone of red (such as carnelian or red jasper) or white (such
   as snowy quartz or angel jasper)

Art, writing, or craft materials (your choice)

Special refreshments (see chapter 8, Preparing the Feast).

Now fill the bathtub with water, and add ingredients that make the water fragrant or cleansing. A cup of apple-cider vinegar gets you squeaky-clean and acts as a natural deodorant and moisturizer! Have your favorite relaxation music playing softly. Light a few votive candles in colorful glass holders, and set them around the bathroom. If you wish, light incense. As you soak in the tub, consciously release all the cares of the day, then the tribulations of the past year. Seek through the recesses of your mind and discover any pain, fear, anger, or disappointment; embody those feelings in a figure of snow; visualize the sun rising and the snow melting in the warmth of returning spring. Let those feelings go, and immediately replace them with emotions, memories, and dreams of the opposite sort: healing where there was pain, courage instead of fear, love to replace anger, hopes realized to banish disappointment.

When you feel clean and content, leave the bath, dry yourself, and put on a clean robe. Enter the ritual room in darkness. Sit and breathe deeply and slowly for a few moments. Now light a single candle, saying:

> *In the midst of darkness, I create light. In the time of cold, I*
> *bring warmth. In the depth of winter, I find the signs of spring.*

Ritually purify the room with Earth and Water (a little salt mixed in water), then Fire and Air (incense). Create a sacred space by casting the circle, with words of your own choosing or these:

> *I conjure thee, O circle of light and power, that thou may be a*
> *boundary between the outer darkness and the inner flame; a*
> *guardian and a protection, to preserve and contain the power*
> *I shall raise within; wherefore, do I bless and consecrate thee!*

Call the Elemental Powers:

Facing East:

> *Powers of Air, I call upon thee. Winter winds, gentle breezes*
> *of spring, come to my circle. Bring the breath of life, and the*
> *inspiration of poets and artists. So mote it be!*

Facing South:

> *Powers of Fire, I call upon thee. Crackling hearthfire, waxing*
> *sunlight, come to my circle. Bring the warmth of the new*
> *season, and the purifying power of your flames. So mote it be!*

Facing West:

> *Powers of Water, I call upon thee. Crystallized snow, trickling*
> *streams of snowmelt, come to my circle. Bring the healing*
> *waters from your sacred springs and holy wells. So mote it be!*

Facing North:

> *Powers of Earth, I call upon thee. Fallow fields, first buds of tree*
> *and flower, come to my circle. Bring the knowledge of smith and*
> *artisan, the skill to shape metal and matter. So mote it be!*

In your own words, invite Brigit, the great Celtic triple goddess of healing, inspiration, and smithcraft, to your circle. You may also wish to invite the male aspect of divinity; one good choice would be the Dagda, the "Good Father" and god of protection and abundance.

Now be seated before the altar, and ask the Three Blessings of Brigit:

Healing: Think about your health. Resolve to take specific steps to heal any part of you that needs it; write them down. Take up the chalice, salute Brigit, say "I ask for Your blessing of Healing," and drink it down. Light a second candle on the altar.

Inspiration: What project or problem faces you that requires inspiration? Where do you need ideas, insights, and understanding? Speak your need aloud. Lift the incense burner (carefully, if it's hot), waft some of the smoke toward your face and inhale gently, then say "I ask for Your blessing of Inspiration." Light another candle on the altar.

Craft: Meditate on what you want to create in the season ahead. A work of art, a piece of furniture, a new skill such as cooking or competence with a computer? Speak aloud (and write down) the first three steps you will take to achieve it. Look at the item on your altar that represents something you have already made or achieved, and remember how you did it. Take the small red or white stone and say, "I ask for your blessing of Smithcraft." Light another candle. Carry the stone with you until you have met your goal.

Stand, and speak these words:

> *Three blessings have I asked, and now I ask one more. Brigit,*
> *goddess of sovereignty who grants power to kings, grant that I*

may have rulership over myself: my own imagination, my will,

my emotions, my body, and my life, that I may do my part to

make all blessings real. So mote it be! (Light the fifth candle.)

Now celebrate in the way that feels best to you: write a poem, make something with your hands, dance, enjoy refreshments, or whatever you wish. When you are about ready for sleep, say farewell to the Elemental powers, thank Brigit, and open the circle.

Carefully extinguish all the candles and incense, both in the bathroom and where you held your ritual. Retire to bed, and sleep well.

Celebrating with Your Family

On February 1, the best cooks of the family should begin creating a feast from the recipes in this book, or your own favorites. That evening each member of the family should bathe and put on brightly colored, festive clothes. Decorate the front door and living room or dining room with red and white, and both pine boughs and flowers to show the coming transition from winter to spring. Prepare a tray with a small evergreen brush, a bowl of salt water, and a dozen or so small pieces of rose quartz.

Then gather around a big table or on the floor and create a Brigit doll from corn husks (or straw), scraps of fabric, and ribbon (see chapter 3). While one or two people are creating the doll, others can decorate "Bride's Bed"—a basket decked with ribbons and flowers (see pp. 64–65)—or make the wand to lie next to her. Your best storyteller should tell tales and legends about Brigit as you work.

When Brigit is in her bed by the fireside, or in some central cozy place, one member of the family should take the part of Brigit, going out the back and around to the front door. She may dress in white and red, and even wear a crown of candles (see the instructions in chapter 3 so it's done safely). When she knocks, everyone should throw open the door and shout, "Welcome, Brigit!" and invite her into the warmth.

The oldest unmarried girl picks up the tray to attend her, and they begin to walk widdershins (counterclockwise) through the house, beginning just inside the front door, as she blesses the house and everyone in it. At each doorway, she uses the small evergreen bough to sprinkle the four sides of the doorway with salt water while reciting, "Blessed be they who pass through this door, both in their coming in and their going out."

She sprinkles a few drops of water on each wall, and in each closet, fireplace, etc. At each window she sprinkles the four sides of the window frame, saying, "Blessed be the visions seen through this window, and the fresh air and light that enter this home."

At each interior corner of the house she places a rose quartz, saying, "Peace and safety and health be unto all who dwell within this home." At each exterior door she makes a sweeping motion from inside to outside with the evergreen brush, saying, "All that would harm, begone!"

She then sprinkles the threshold, saying, "All that enter be pure and good!" Finally, on either side of the doorway, she places a piece of rose quartz, saying, "May all that enter this blessed home do so with peace in their hearts."

When they return to the front door, she instructs the family (and any friends present) to step out of the door before she does the door blessing. After the door is blessed and the rose quartz in place, the family members re-enter the house, one at a time,

and she blesses each one by sprinkling them with a little bit of salt water and saying, "May your heart be always peaceful and joyous within these walls. Blessed be
you (Name), now and always, forever in the sight of the Lady and the Lord. So
mote it be!" She is led to the feast, and offered the first choice of all that is laid out
before her.

Then it's time for the feast! Maybe you'll have some *really* old-fashioned dishes
like roast rabbit or venison onion soup, colcannon, and braided bread. You may
indulge in a bottle of mead, some mulled cider, hot herbal teas, or a glass of syllabub. Possibly you'll prefer more modern dishes such as chili and corn bread,
with ice cream for dessert.

If you need a break between supper and dessert, you might play the Candle
Game, as described in chapter 3.

Later in the evening, adults and older children may want to do some divination
about the coming year, using the wax-in-water method, or a Tarot reading, or bib-
liomancy (see chapter 4). Give one another blessings when it's finally time to
sleep, such as this traditional Irish blessing: "May you be kept safe and warm
under Brigit's mantle." And don't forget to say "goodnight" to Brigit in her bed!

A Small Group Ritual:
The Mysteries of Smithcraft

This ritual is best held at the full moon, in the evening during the planetary hour
of Mars. However, there's only a one-in-twenty-eight chance that February 2 will
have a full moon, so do it on February 2 anyway.

Gather a leather apron, hammer, and tongs, and iron objects such as old horseshoes, and place them on or beside the altar. If you can find a bellows and anvil,
they would be excellent additions. Then find or create images of the smith-gods
(Brigit, Wayland, Hephaestus, Vulcan), and place them on a red or orange altar
cloth with the other items. The altar should have on it:

Two candles to represent Goddess and God

A bowl of water and dish of salt

Incense in a censer

A sword or athame

And at the base of the altar:

Drums and rattles

A boombox with quiet music

Build a second altar of stones, with a charcoal fire in it, to represent the forge; and four simple quarter altars with crafts materials on them, for the participants to create talismans later:

- Have small discs of copper, into which runes can be hammered with a hammer and small chisel.

- Make pottery clay available; symbols can be incised with simple tools such as paring knives and toothpicks, and the clay kiln-fired later. Or use hobby clay that can be hardened in an ordinary oven.

- Get scraps of leather and let people stamp symbols and runes into them.

- Use sculptable metal, so that everyone can mold or impress whatever images they wish.

- Saw thin cross-sections of wood from a branch 1–2 inches in diameter, and have a wood-burning tool available for adding the symbols.

- Obtain some shells of about the same size, plus model paints and hobby brushes.

- For pocket-piece talismans, small flat river pebbles can be collected and symbols painted on them.

As participants gather, help them to become centered by hammering rhythmically on the forge or any piece of iron. Encourage everyone to chime in with drums, rattles, and other musical instruments. Let the rhythm go on until it naturally wanes and stops.

The Smith, or one of them if the ritual is led by a team, purifies the area and participants with liberal splashes of salt water.

Cast the circle using an athame or sword and the following words:

I conjure thee, O circle of fire and metal, be thou the boundary between the world of humanity and the Smithy of the Gods! Guard and protect our Craft and the power we shall raise within! Wherefore do I bless and consecrate thee.

Call the Elemental powers with words such as these:

Facing the East:

Powers of Air, Guardians of the Watchtowers of the East, winds that fan the fires of the forge, winds that cool the brow of the Smith, winds of the ancient knowledge of smithcraft, of metals, and of stones, come to this circle tonight. So mote it be!

Facing the South:

Powers of Fire, Guardians of the Watchtowers of the South, flame of forge that heats the iron, flame which melts apart and welds together, flame that transforms the metal that it may be worked, flame which hardens so that all else will yield before its sharpness and strength, come to this circle tonight. So mote it be!

Facing the West:

Powers of Water, Guardians of the Watchtowers of the West, liquid that quenches the hot metal to temper it, cool draught which quenches thirst after the heat of the forge, cleanliness of the ritual bath, come to this circle tonight. So mote it be!

Facing the North:

Powers of Earth, Guardians of the Watchtowers of the North, minerals of the earth, steel and stone, wood and bronze, gold and charcoal, hammer and anvil, sword and shield, helm and torc, enduring matter that was before and will endure after all else is passed, come to this circle tonight. So mote it be!

Invoke the goddess Brigit:

> *Great Lady, Exalted One, King-maker, Bright Arrow, we call*
> *upon You; Brigit of the eternal flame, Brigit of the sacred*
> *springs, mistress of poets, healers, and smiths; we invite You*
> *to our circle; enter and give us Your blessings.*

Invoke the god Wayland:

> *Lord of Smithcraft, Mighty Arm, Sword-maker, Tool-forger, we*
> *call upon You; Wayland of the spectral smithy, Wayland of the*
> *forest forge, master of craftsmen, artisans, and smiths; we invite*
> *You to our circle; enter and give us Your blessings.*

Now invite the participants to meditate. Introduce the activity as follows:

> *Know this: each of us crafts our life from the raw materials*
> *given us by the gods. Some of us are born with clever hands and*
> *fine materials, others have less to work with; yet with learning*
> *and practice and hard work, any of us can craft a life that is*
> *beautiful and worthy to present before the Mighty Ones. For*
> *did not the gods create the very universe from nothing but the*
> *original void? And are we not ourselves the children of the gods?*

> *Therefore, tonight we ask each of you to meditate silently, and*
> *to resolve on some action you can take that will make your life*
> *better. As a sign of your resolve, and a reminder, and a magickal*
> *tool to help you carry through, you will have the opportunity to*
> *make a talisman within this circle. At the quarters are people to*
> *help you with clay, or metal, or leather, or wood and other*
> *materials. Choose one, and place upon it the symbol of your*
> *intent. Think now on what you will do, and when the bell*
> *chimes, go to any quarter and begin.*

Station a helper at each quarter of the circle, each with different materials and tools on hand. They should have papers with various symbols: runes, astrological and alchemical signs, simple designs of animals and plants, etc. After a couple of minutes, the bell is rung and each person comes forward to create their own talisman from the materials provided.

During the crafting of the talismans, have music or soft drumming.

When all are done, everyone stands and re-forms the circle. One at a time, each person steps forward and proclaims the purpose of their talisman in a loud voice, and asks the blessings of the gods on it. For example: "I present before the gods a talisman of healing! Brigit and Wayland, bless this talisman!" Each proclamation should be followed by a drum roll and cheers.

Then each person should wear or hold their talisman, as a circle dance begins to raise power and charge them. Let the drumming rise to a crescendo, then stop, and ask all to pour the energy into the objects they made. Afterwards, make sure that everyone sends any excess energy into the Earth.

Celebrate with cakes and wine or juice, or with hearty bread and cheese, and sparkling cider or ale to wash it down. Thank the gods for their bounty, bless the food and drink, and pass it deosil (clockwise) around the circle. As each person passes it on, they should offer a blessing or wish to the recipient.

Open the circle with farewells to the Elemental powers and thanks to the gods and goddesses of smithcraft. Release the energy of the circle into the talismans, and say, "The circle is open, but never broken. Merry meet, and merry part, and merry meet again!" Then enjoy music and feasting.

A Community Celebration: The Three Faces of Brigit

This is designed as a community celebration, with a couple of dozen or more people in attendance. You will need to hire a roomy hall or public meeting room, perhaps from a church, library, or local government.

Prepare by gathering materials and setting up the temple. Across one end of the room, about six feet from the wall, hang a white curtain that reaches from the floor to above head height. Behind the curtain near the wall, place candles so that the figures behind the fabric will be back-lit.

In the main part of the room, set up an altar, with the usual tools, plus a tall, white pillar candle, and before it place a medium-sized to large cauldron. Have water on hand and a container with dry ice, to create a mist effect in the cauldron. Practice before the ritual to see how much water and dry ice will create the effect you desire. On the other side of the altar put another cauldron, tray, or pot half-filled with sand. Into it place candles of several colors—enough for each participant in the ritual.

At the far end of the room place three chairs to serve as thrones for the three aspects of Brigit. You can cover them loosely with fabric of three different colors. Beside each throne, place a large white candle, matching the one on the altar, and some wooden matches. The room layout should look like this:

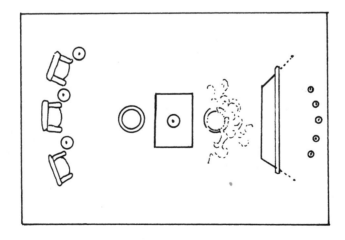

Three women will play the role of Brigit in her three aspects. They should all wear simple white robes, but the first also has a green cloak for poetry and inspiration; the second a red cloak for fire and smithcraft; and the third a blue or white cloak for water and healing. In addition, the first wears a battery-powered crown of candles, unlit at first, and carries a staff or scepter; the second carries a hammer and a sword; and the third carries a caduceus and a chalice.

The ritual should begin with the room lit only by the white candle on the altar. Have the leaders cast the circle, then place the dry ice in the cauldron to create mist, while participants wait outside the room. Behind the curtain, the three Brigits wait standing in line, one behind another. In this way they will appear as one silhouette when the candles behind them are lit.

When they are ready, the leaders should open a gateway and welcome each person into the room and the circle with these words:

> *By the power of the Living Flame, I welcome you to this*
> *sacred circle.*

Everyone sits, and a leader blows out the altar candle and speaks:

> *Last autumn, we watched the nights grow longer, and embraced*
> *darkness and silence of winter. Now the fields lie fallow, the sun*
> *is dim in the pale sky, and the cold lingers. In this season it is*
> *hard to remember the warmth and light and new life of spring;*
> *but they come. They come. The Goddess reminds us that winter*
> *is not forever. Brigit reminds us.*

Now stirring music begins quietly, then swells. Behind the curtain the third Brigit, closest to the candles, lights them, and the silhouette of the first Brigit is thrown on the gauzy fabric. She raises her arms and speaks:

Brigit 1 speaks:

> *I am Brigit, Queen of the Slim Fairy Folk, Elder Goddess of the*
> *Fomorians and Mother of the Tuatha de Danaan, Exalted Lady;*
> *and before the beginning of days, I was. I am also Song-sweet*

> *Brigit of the Tribe of the Green Mantles, and I sent songs and*
> *music on the wind before ever the bells of the chapels were rung*
> *in the West or heard in the East. I am the heart of poetry, and I*
> *have been a breath in your mind since before your first birth.*

Brigit 2 steps from behind the first and moves to her side, so that she casts a separate shadow. She speaks:

> *I am Brigantia, the Eternal Flame, Mistress of the Secrets of the*
> *Forge; and I shape the world with iron and fire. And I am the*
> *Warrior Queen of the Brigantes, Leader of the Immortal Host,*
> *Defender of the Clans, the Victorious One. And the day has*
> *dawned that will see me coming into the hearts of men and*
> *women like a flame upon dry grass, like a flame of wind in a*
> *great wood, like a flame of justice that will reach the very*
> *heavens!*

Brigit 3 then steps from behind the first and moves to her other side, saying:

> *I am Bride of the Isles, the Lady of the Sea, Conception of the*
> *Waves, the Healing Power of Pure Love. I am the sacred chalice*
> *that contains the mystery of life, I am the crystal waters of the*
> *holy wells, and I am the white foam on the breast of the rushing*
> *rivers in springtime. In the Land of Eternal Youth my name is*
> *Mountain-traveler; and in the Country of Ancient Years it is*
> *Seek-Beyond. My womb brings you forth, My waters refresh*
> *you, My touch makes you whole.[2]*

The ritual leader leads a call and response chant:

> *Fire of the heart,*
> *Fire of the mind,*
> *Fire of the hearth,*
> *Fire of the wind,*

Fire of the Art,
Fire out of time!

All: *"She shines for all, she burns in all!"*[3]

When the chant climaxes, all three Brigits turn, and proceed from behind the curtain. The last blows out the candles behind them. They walk in darkness to the thrones at the other end of the room, and are seated.

The ritual leader again lights the candle on the altar. We won't require that you use flint and steel, but please use matches—the ancients did not have sacred lighters. The leader says:

> *For more than nine hundred years the flame of Brigit burned*
> *in her shrine at Kildare, tended first by the priestesses of the*
> *goddess, and then by the Catholic sisters of the saint. In the year*
> *1220 the bishop ordered it extinguished* (blows out candle).
> *Soon it was relit* (lights it). *It burned until the Reformation,*
> *during the reign of King Henry the Eighth, and was*
> *extinguished again, and the abbey was destroyed* (blows out
> candle). *In 1996 the flame was lit again in Kildare,* (lights
> candle). *The darkness of ignorance and fear may well put*
> *it out again one day* (blows it out). *But the true flame was*
> *not in Ireland; the true flame is the Goddess* (all three Brigits
> simultaneously light identical candles), *and her fire is*
> *never lost.*
>
> *We invite each of you to take a small candle from this cauldron,*
> *and go to one of the three aspects of Brigit. Light your candle*
> *from her flame, and ask her blessing.*

Play soft music or lead a repetitive chant as people go up to the thrones. The Brigits should have blessings ready to offer as they light the candles, such as these:

Know that within you is an invincible flame; have courage.

*May you find my holy well, and drink of its waters, and be
healed.*

NOTE: If the women acting the part of Brigit are able to channel messages from
the Goddess, or actually aspect Her—that is, take on her persona and speak as
Her—then you may invite participants to quietly voice their cares and problems to
Her, and receive counsel. This will also depend on the size of the group, and how
many want to do this. In a large group, it is better to keep to simple blessings.

When all have visited Brigit, invite people to put their candles in the sand cauldron or tray of sand, remembering which is their candle. With drumming and
song, raise power to further charge the candles for whatever qualities people
want—purification, healing, courage, skill, self-mastery, and so on. Here is a chant
that might be used (to the tune of the chant, ". . . Like a drop of rain. . . ."):

We all come from the Goddess, and to her we shall return,
Like a tongue of flame, reaching to the sky above!
Repeat as desired.

When the power peaks, stop and channel the energy into the candles; then
release any excess power into the Earth.

Now it's time to share cakes and wine—
but since we are honoring Brigit, it would
be more appropriate to pass a platter of rye
bread and goat's cheese, and a tankard of
Irish beer (or sparkling apple juice for non-
drinkers). Let these be blessed by the three
Brigits in turn, and as each person passes
them to their neighbor, they offer a blessing
along with the food.

Then bid the four Elements farewell,
and offer your thanks to the Brigits, who
process back behind the curtain to divest
themselves of their accouterments and

become normal people for the party. Close by holding hands and offering a benediction:

> *May the holy maiden Bride, radiant flame of gold,*
> *Protect you from all dangers.*
> *No fire, no sun, no moon will burn you,*
> *No lake, no water, no sea shall drown you,*
> *No arrow of fairy nor dart of fay shall wound you,*
> *May Brigit's waters heal you.*
> *May Brigit's winds inspire you.*
> *May Brigit's fire warm you.*
> *Under her protection, go in peace.*[4]

Now let everyone sing, feast, or find quiet corners for divination.

Some Additional Ideas for Rituals

There are so many customs and activities from the lore of this holiday that you may be hard put to choose among them! Here are some other activities that could be included in a celebratory ritual (many are explained in more detail in chapter 3).

- Hold a torchlit procession around the property or the neighborhood.

- Perform a symbolic cleansing in which participants toss notes onto the floor representing what they wish to remove from their lives (crumple them first), and the Priestess sweeps them up and burns them in a cauldron.

- Banish the winter season by bringing out the Yule greenery (such as pine wreaths, swags, or boughs from the tree), and burning it. Obviously if this is done indoors, it must be done with great care, in a fireplace. If you have only a cauldron to burn things in, you can burn a few symbolic twigs and take the rest to a nearby woods to leave as natural compost.

- Crown Brigit with her crown of candles. This can be made more dramatic by announcing some of her titles, as listed in chapter 2.

- Try a spiral dance, where participants hold hands and the leader takes them into a tighter circle, then reversing, out again. Some groups do this as a "meeting dance," where participants kiss as they pass face-to-face, but we have found that some people don't want to kiss relative strangers, and further that it's hard to kiss properly if the line is moving quickly.

- Simple folk dances are easy to learn, or try a dance where men and women link arms and dance back to back. This can be hilarious fun, as it is not easy to do gracefully!

- Starhawk suggests that "Coveners share their creative work—poetry, songs, art works, stories, crafts. Those who are not artistic might share something about their work—a plan that materialized, a good idea, a special accomplishment. The Goddess is thanked for her inspiration."[5]

- Weave a *Crios Bhríde* or woven ring of straw during the ritual (explained in chapter 3), and have everyone step through it three times (right foot first) for good fortune in the coming year.

- You can hold a candle-making workshop during the afternoon before the ritual, and then have participants bring their new candles to be anointed, consecrated, blessed, or decorated during the ritual. This works best with ice candles—others may not have set in so few hours.

- If you have a great story-teller available to you, ask them to come and tell legends and tales about Brigit by candlelight.

- Gather some horseshoes from a local stable, a farrier, or antique shops; clean them well. During the ritual, pass them through a flame and ask Brigit's blessing on them, then distribute them to participants who can be instructed to hang the horseshoes over a doorway at home (horns up to hold the luck) as a talisman from the goddess of smithcraft. If you wish, you can also hand out ribbons, silk flowers, and tiny bells; then everyone can take a few minutes to decorate them.

- Hand out seeds or seedlings that can be nurtured during the last weeks of winter, and then transplanted outdoors as soon as the weather is good.

- Dim the lights, put on some gentle music, and lead everyone in a guided meditation to visit Brigit. If young children are present, you will have to judge whether they can sit still for a quiet event like this. A meditation narrative is included at the end of this chapter, and you can adapt it in any way you like.

Conclusion

Remember that half the fun of a holiday celebration is planning it, gathering the materials, and setting it up. The more people you involve in the process, the less work and more fun it is for everyone. And if your celebration will include children, remember to give them roles in the ritual as well; a child who gets to wear a costume, distribute cookies, or put up decorations will remember the event with smiles for a long time . . . as will the adults!

A Meditation at the End of Winter

You stand in the forest as the lingering warmth of autumn departs . . . the leaves around you are hazy gold and nut-brown, with the darker evergreens lending contrast. The air is cool, and the scent of wood smoke fills the air.

As you walk along a narrow path, you notice that the sky is growing darker, and the chill becomes sharper. A rose and gold sunset flames in the west, while the eastern sky shades toward midnight blue. A few snowflakes sift down through the twilight, but you press on. The snowfall thickens and the trees are skeletal black shapes in the night; and all is very quiet; there is only the muffled crunch of your boots in the newfallen snow.

It occurs to you that autumn has silently departed with the sun, and that you have crossed some subtle boundary and entered the kingdom of winter. Darkness surrounds you, and the snow keeps falling. After a time, your patient trudging brings you to the edge of the woods, and you look out over a sweeping white landscape of hills and vales, illumined only by starlight and a slender crescent moon. In the far distance, rugged mountains tower into the sky, their icy peaks glowing with faint moonlight.

When your eyes return to the rolling drifts that stretch between you and the mountains, you notice a tiny, flickering red light in the distance. It seems to promise hospitality; you imagine a warm fireside and a pot of hot soup simmering over the flames. Behind you is only the cold, black forest; you set off across the snowclad land.

It seems that you walk forever, in an immensity of sky and snow and silence. You cannot tell if the tiny light is closer; in time, you stop looking, and just walk through the growing drifts.

You awaken to a pale dawn, lying on the ground, and realize that you must have lost consciousness in the night. You are feeling stiff, but amazed that you didn't freeze to death. Then you suddenly realize that you aren't cold at all, and that you are resting on grass, not snow. Before you is an ancient well, surrounded by moss-covered stones; incredibly, flowers cluster at its base. The air is warm. When you lift your eyes, you realize that you are in the center of the snow-filled valley, with the mountains still looming in the distance; but the snow stops a few yards away, as at an invisible boundary. It is an oasis of warmth and life. Words read long ago come to mind: "In the midst of winter, I found within myself an invincible summer."

When you move to the well, you see that its waters are clear; a tiny spotted fish swims within. A voice, husky but feminine, fills your mind: "First, you must heal; mind and heart, body and soul. Ask for whatever you need, and then partake of My waters and know wholeness." You think for a long moment, and then whisper your pain to the Goddess. You drink, and it is as though all weariness and hurt fall away from you, leaving you refreshed, renewed, young, and filled with joy.

As the sun rises in a clear blue sky, you walk on, deeper into the snow. Glancing behind, you can no longer see the green glade of the well, but its effects still sing in your blood and bones. However, the mountains seem no closer than they were.

As the sun moves toward the horizon, you become aware of a tower in the distance. It appears very tall, but its pure white stone was lost in the snowy landscape until now. A few more minutes of brisk walking brings you much closer, and now you see that its walls are carved with graceful curves and arabesques, and the shapes of intricate crystals and fantastic creatures. It soars to the sky, yet seems so delicate that it might be a spire transplanted from the faery realm itself. An open door seems to welcome you; and you enter.

Within the tower, rays of sunlight slant from high, arched windows, light so rich and golden that it seems a material thing. Beneath your feet are soft, deep carpets in jeweled tones, and the chamber is filled with art: sculptures so perfectly shaped they seem alive, paintings and wall hangings telling the stories of myth and legend, fabrics too rich and fluid for mortal royalty. And there are stairs, spiraling round the wall and up into a lavender dimness. You move up them.

At the top, you find a chamber filled with exquisite rugs and cushions, and a small circular table where incense curls from a bronze vessel. Again, the voice sounds in your mind: "Now, you may seek your dreams and visions. Breathe the fragrance before you, and cast yourself upon the wind." Reality shifts and flows about you, and you find yourself standing in the casement of an open window, looking at the ground far below. The snow crystals sparkle in the last rays of sunlight as you step forward, fall . . . and fly. You feel the wind beneath your wings, and your eyesight is keener than you imagined possible. You begin to search the world for dreams.

Later, you regain consciousness to find yourself sitting in a snowdrift. The sun has set and the stars are emerging. You wonder if you dreamed the flight until you notice that all around you the snow is virgin; there are no footprints leading to the place where you crouch.

In the distance, at the base of the looming mountains, is the tiny flicker of red light that you saw—was it only yesterday? You stand, and walk on toward it. Tonight it appears that your efforts will be rewarded. The light grows closer over the next hours, and by midnight you can actually see flames. The flames are visible through the open front of a roughhewn shed of logs; they are the flames of a forge, and next to it you can see a great black anvil with a leather apron draped across it. The tools of a metalworker hang from the walls.

*You enter the shed, and feel moved to put on the leather apron
and pick up a hammer. The warmth of the forge feels good
after your long, cold trek, and the flames seem cheerful and
welcoming. The hammer feels good in your hand. At this
moment, the voice sounds in your mind once again: "Now, it is
time to create. Use the tools at hand to make your vision into a
thing of iron and sweat. Carry it to remind you that day by day,
minute by minute, you create reality. You are the smith, forging
your own destiny."*

*An image comes to your mind, and your hands move of their
own accord, selecting the raw stock, pumping the bellows,
hammering the iron. You work through the night—inspired,
tireless. The shed is very warm; you perspire copiously and
drink great drafts of water from a copper dipper hanging in a
barrel. The hours fly by as the focus of your will takes shape in
the fire and on the anvil. Dawn breaks as you polish the sword
you have made; powerful and elegant, supple and quick, it
feels as though it has always been part of you. The rays of the
morning sun flash from the blade. Gradually you become
aware of the world beyond the forge; the snow is gone, birds
sing, a cool breeze blows across the waving grass, and bright
wildflowers appear before you. In the night, spring has arrived.*

*From the east, out of the sun, a woman walks toward you. The
light gathers around her until all the radiance seems to emanate
from her body. She is tall and golden-haired, wearing a simple
white robe and a brilliant green cloak that billows behind her.
Flowers spring up where she has trod. She speaks, and you
recognize the voice that has been with you through your long
journey: "You know Me. I am the fount of healing, the source of*

inspiration, the flames of the forge. And I am she who crowns the sovereign of the land. You have established your rulership over the greatest territory ever known: your own heart, and mind, and spirit. In token of this, I knight you with your own sword." She reaches out her hand; and you give her the sword. As you kneel, she touches you on each shoulder with the blade, and a thrill runs through you from the places where the sword has touched.

"And I crown you with a crown of light." In her hands is a glowing circlet of pure light, brilliant white and warm golden, and somehow radiant with all the colors of the rainbow. She places it on your brow and joy fills you. "Bless you, sovereign of your own spirit." When you stand, she is no longer visible. But you know where she is; she is in your heart.

Breathe deeply now, and take the images and feelings of this journey into your memory and your body. When you are ready, let your consciousness return to this place and this time, bearing with you all that you have felt and learned. Blessed be.

Notes

1. Marian Green, *A Calendar of Festivals*, p. 17.
2. Adapted from Fiona MacLeod, *Winged Destiny*.
3. Starhawk, *Spiral Dance*, pp. 174–175.
4. Adapted from John O'Donovan, trans., *The Martyrology of Donegal*.
5. Starhawk, p. 187.

Additional ritual outlines for the season can be found in the following books, listed in the bibliography:

Pauline Campanelli, *The Wheel of the Year*.

Janet and Stewart Farrar, *Eight Sabbats for Witches*.

Amber K, *Covencraft*.

Starhawk, *The Spiral Dance*.

The Candles of Candle-Mass

Candlelight creates mood. From the eerie flicker of a candle stub clutched in the hand of a child exploring a "haunted house," to the mellow glow of slim white tapers at a romantic dinner, to the splendor of vast candelabra blazing in a cathedral; candles do something for the human imagination that modern lighting cannot hope to achieve. And one thing that candles do, in seasons dark and cold, is to serve as tiny reminders of the greater light and life-giving warmth that comes from the sun.

The earliest lights were torches, rushlights (rushes dipped in fat), and oil lamps. The first candles combined a wick with a tube of wax, oil, or fat that was hard at room temperature. The Egyptians had candles with papyrus wicks, and the Hindus skimmed fat off boiling cinnamon to make non-animal-fat candles—wouldn't that smell wonderful! But the most common candles were tallow—wicks dipped in fat from slaughtered animals, and very smelly. Fragrant beeswax candles were always the most expensive and few could afford them.

The word "candle" or "candela" came to the English language in about the eighth century C.E., from the Latin *candeo*, "to burn." It was an ecclesiastical term: candles were not something found in the average cottage, but were a liturgical tool reserved for the churches.

To the Church, the candle was invested with great symbolism. Church candles were and are made mostly from beeswax (medieval scientists thought that bees were virginal, as indeed some are) to represent the flesh of Jesus, born from a virgin. The wick symbolized the soul of Jesus himself, and the flame was divinity. Candles are used at almost every function from baptisms to excommunications, and in fact the mass may not be said without having lighted candles.

In some of the great cathedrals of medieval Europe, the lighting arrangements were ornate and splendid. Magnificent chandeliers were crafted of copper, silver, and gold. The Emperor Constantine designed the Lateran basilica to have 8,730 candles. We read of great, branched, bronze *candelabra aurichalca* that were ten and even eighteen feet high, and fifteen feet across. Some were shaped as crosses, trees, crowns, or even animals.

The faithful burn candles at shrines when they wish to offer thanks or ask for intercession. In the Middle Ages there was a custom called "measuring to," which meant to offer to a saint a candle (or candles) as tall as the person for whom the favor was desired. (For example: "I'll measure to Saint Brigid, and perhaps she'll help me with a healing.")

Of course, many other faiths have also employed candles in their rituals. In times of old, at the festival of Imbolg, candles were lit to symbolize the growing light and lengthening days, and to encourage the sun in his ascent. You can create and decorate your own candles with this symbolism in mind, or for specific magickal spells, or "just for pretty."

Simplest of all is to purchase candles at a store and then decorate them with pine twigs, stones, shells, seeds, flowers, berries, and ribbon around the bases, and perhaps designs drawn with glue and covered with glitter.

That's the short version of candle-making, but since one of the central themes of Candlemas is candles, why not make your own? The grocery or hobby store will have blocks of paraffin, or you can recycle stubs of old and broken candles, or with luck you might find a source of beeswax, which burns with a wonderful smell. Look for honey producers in your area, and call.

What's in a Candle?

Most candles today are made of paraffin, also known as petroleum wax, available at any crafts shop. A 10-pound block of paraffin will make about four quarts of melted wax. It is graded according to its melting point (more about this later). Beeswax is expensive, and requires a fairly thick wick when it is used by itself. However, it mixes well with paraffin, and the resulting candle will burn longer and drip less. A few other natural waxes are available, such as bayberry. Waxes can be mixed together, and after melting will stay homogenized enough for the candle to cool without looking odd.

If you are a beginning candle-maker, start with paraffin and then try a beeswax blend. But at some point, you may want to get audacious and try making candles of bayberry wax—if you are lucky enough to live in an area where bayberries grow!

Make the wax in late fall when the bayberries are ripe. Pick several quarts of the ripe, gray berries for each large candle (1½ quarts per 8-inch taper). At home, pick over the berries, removing any stems and leaves; cover the berries with water and simmer for an hour. Let the mixture cool overnight; the wax will float to the top in a large disk. It will still have bits of berry skin and twig, so melt it again in a double boiler with a little water. In small batches, strain the wax and water through muslin into a bowl. Let this batch harden, and if there are still impurities, repeat the process until the wax is clean. Dry the wax and keep it tightly wrapped in tissue paper inside plastic wrap, in a cool place away from light. Natural bayberry scent is elusive and fades quickly.

When February rolls around and it's time to create your candles, use the wax in any of the following "recipes." For a *very* subtle fragrance, mix the bayberry wax with other waxes. Try a bayberry/beeswax combination for a special treat!

For the bayberry fragrance without all the work, buy one bayberry candle from a hobby shop, and cut it into pieces. Commercial bayberry candles are so intensely, artificially perfumed that they can drive you out of the room; blending a small piece with each batch of wax you melt will give you a delicately fragranced candle that smells more natural than the commercial one.

Back to melting points. Adding 5 to 30 percent stearine per pound of wax increases the melting point, making the candle harder, so it burns longer and drips less. Stearine, or stearic acid, is an additive found at craft supply stores. Stearine also makes the candle more opaque, so if you want to see through the wax (perhaps to cubes of another color embedded in the candle) you may be willing to have a lower melting point. Stearine also darkens dye colors, so those cubes inside will be more visible if you add stearine to them when you make them, before assembling the whole candle.

Never melt wax over an open flame. Use a double boiler or a slow-cooker. Wax melted in a pot directly over flames will create vapors that will ignite. Keep powdered baking soda and a large frying pan lid at hand to smother any flames. And never drip water into melted wax (especially not to put out a wax fire!); the combination will explode like water in hot grease.

The melting points of various waxes are:

Bayberry	113–114.8 degrees F
Beeswax	144–147 degrees F
Candelilla	154–158 degrees F
Paraffin	118–165 degrees F
Stearine	131 or 161 degrees F

A candy thermometer is a very handy tool to have when making candles. Stir the wax constantly while it is melting.

Want colored candles? Neither fabric dyes nor broken wax crayons will work; use only dyes that are made especially for candlemaking. These come in liquid form or as solid cakes or pellets. Add them a little at a time, after the stearine has completely melted and just before the wax is molded or dipped. Test the intensity of the dye by dropping a few drops of wax on waxed paper, over a sheet of white paper. Remember, the candle will be thick, not just a thin layer; so take the time to let the drops cool and add a few more layers on top of the first test drops, to check the wax opacity and color intensity. It sounds complicated, but these aren't just any old candles—they're *your* special holiday candles, so you want to do it right.

You may want to add a fragrance. Natural perfumes are more delicate than artificial perfumes, and any essential oil can be used to perfume a candle. Either use ¼ ounce of oil per 3 pounds of wax, or saturate the wick in oil before pouring or dipping the candle. Add the scent just before dipping or pouring, as long exposure to heat may alter the scent. If your candle looks mottled, you may have used too much perfume oil. Remelt the candle and add more wax. Or enjoy the mottled effect—and the cloud of perfume!

You will probably want a wick; candles work better with wicks. (The authors are Wiccan, and once someone said to us, "Are you some of them Wickers I heard about?" To which the only possible reply is, "Yeah, we make candles—what of it?") Anyway; use only commercial wicks from a craft store. The supplies you need can also be ordered on the internet; use "candle supplies" as your search words. Wicking comes in several thread counts and either flat or square-braided. A good rule of thumb for sizing: if the candle diameter is:

1–3 inches	use wick size	15-ply
4-inch or tapers	use wick size	24-ply
over 4 inches	use wick size	30-ply

The melting point of the wax and any additives used may affect the outcome, too. Try one and see if it burns well.

Wire wicks have, as the name implies, a very thin wire in them. These are good for molded candles where the candle is being poured right-side up, and the wick needs to stand upright in the empty mold. Those little square metal pieces found at the bottom of many molded candles are called wick holders, and are useful for holding wire wicking in place in an empty mold before you pour in the wax. Wire wicks burn more slowly and provide less light than standard wicking: great for a night-light or seven-day candle, but not so good for "lamps of art" (ritual candles) on your altar.

How to Make a Candle

A simple dip taper. Now that you have the ingredients, let's make a candle. The simplest, oldest method is dipping, in which a piece of wicking is dipped repeatedly into a tub of melted wax. For dipping candles, you will need:

Wax

Stearine, if desired

A double boiler for melting the wax

A spoon for stirring

A candy thermometer

Dyes and scents, if desired

A tall, deep pot for dipping in

Wicking

A stick or dowel rod to tie the wicking to

A place to let the candles hang to cool—two kitchen chairs back to back work well, with a pole between them and newspapers underneath to catch drips.

Tie one end of a piece of wicking around a stick; it should be the length of your candle plus 1½ inches. If you are dipping two or more candles, cut the wicking twice the length of the candles, plus 3 inches, and tie them to the stick with two half-hitches so the wicks are about two inches apart.

After the first dip or two, pull the wick to straighten it, then allow the candle to cool thoroughly between dippings.

Wax temperature is important, because wax that is too cool will clump on the candle, and wax that is too hot will melt off the previous layer. Dipping wax should be 165–170 degrees. As the candles are dipped, the bottom ends will naturally become larger than the top of the candle, hence the name "taper." Dip until the diameter half an inch above the fattest part of the candle fits the size of the candleholder you will be using. Let the finished tapers cool overnight, then cut off the base ends at the fattest part with a sharp knife dipped in hot water, and trim the bases to fit the candleholder. This way you will get a cylindrical base and the candle will stand straight and firm in the candleholder, with no wobbling. Trim the wicks to about ½ inch and polish your new candle with a nylon stocking. Or, leave the pairs of candles attached by the wicking, tie them with a bit of raffia, and insert a sprig of evergreen for decoration. Voilà! A lovely gift for a house-warming or initiation.

Candles From Molds

The other major method of making candles is to mold them in a pre-cast form. Most candles today are made by molding, from simple tapers and votive candles to those huge multi-wicked candles that take four people to lift.

For making molded candles, you will need:

Wax

Stearine, if desired

A double boiler for melting the wax

A spoon for stirring

A candy thermometer

Dyes and scents, if desired

A tall, deep pot for dipping in

Wicking

Molds—bought, found, or made

Silicone spray or peanut oil

A ladle and/or small pitcher

A sheet cake pan

An oven mitt

An ice pick

A long metal rod

A bucket of cool water

Any special items (like ice cubes or a bucket of sand) needed
for the kind of candle you are making.

You can buy candle molds at a hobby shop, along with your other supplies. You don't have to use a store-bought mold, however; a tubular frozen juice container will work splendidly. Also consider using a bucket of slightly damp sand, in which you dig out the shape you want your candle to be. You can even use emptied eggshells.

Before pouring the wax, spray the inside of the mold with a silicone spray, or lightly brush the inside of the mold with peanut oil. This will allow you to remove the hardened candles from their molds easily.

The most common way to get the wick in a molded candle is to put the wick in the mold first, followed by the wax. Most commercial molds fill from the bottom, so your candle is upside-down while you're making it. The mold will have a small hole at the candle's tip. Tie your wick around a toothpick, pull it through the mold from the tip to the open bottom, and tie it to a pencil laid across the open bottom, with the wick taut inside the mold.

Dip the tip-end of the mold in wax two or three times, so the first hot wax you pour in won't shoot out the end on to your shoes. Or use a dab of clay. You can also place the tip-end in a shallow pan of cold water. A little wax may ooze out, but it will harden immediately, and you can add it back to the wax pot later. A sheet cake pan will also catch drips during the pour.

We can't say this too often—melt your wax in a double boiler or slow-cooker, never in a pot that's directly over an open flame, because the vapors can explode. Never heat the wax above 212 degrees, because at 212 degrees it will begin to smoke and turn brown. Never leave melting wax unattended. Add any colors you wish near the end, and the scented oils last. Make sure the wicks are centered in the molds, the molds are in shallow pans to catch wayward drips, and *carefully* pour the wax in. If you need to hold the mold, use an oven mitt. Sometimes it helps to ladle the hot wax into a small pitcher and pour from that. (This part should be done by adults or mature young people under adult supervision, not by children.) For molds made of glass, plastic, cardboard—anything but metal— pour the wax between 150 degrees and 165 degrees. Heat your metal molds to about 100 degrees in the oven before pouring—this will give the candle a smoother finish. Pour wax into metal molds when it is between 190 degrees and 200 degrees.

After the wax is poured into a mold, it will shrink as it cools. This will leave a depression at the top of the mold, or sometimes an air pocket under a thin skin of wax. Break the skin if there is one, then add more wax. You may have to do this more than once to get the surface solid and flat.

Cooling can be hastened by immersing the poured candle in a bucket of cool water, but wait at least half an hour before doing this.

Candles that are 1 inch in diameter should remain in their molds for at least 8 hours, and larger diameter candles will have to cool even longer. Ice candles, explained further on, are an exception.

Some candles are created in "found molds," like eggshells and Yule tree balls, and need to have the wicks put in later. Just skewer the finished candle with a hot ice pick, thread a wire wick in, and backfill the rest of the hole with hot wax. For a longer candle, heat a length of stiff wire, such as the bottom piece of a coat hanger, in place of the ice pick. Wear a leather glove to hold it, so you don't burn yourself.

Egg-shaped candles. Make a mold from an eggshell by punching a small hole in the large end of a raw egg, and cutting out a small circle of eggshell with cuticle scissors. Empty the egg into a bowl and use it for something else, maybe an omelet. Wash the inside of the shell with water, removing the membrane inside. Allow it to dry thoroughly. Place the eggshell hole-side-up in the egg carton and pour in the wax. Allow the wax to set overnight, then carefully chip the shell away. Skewer the candle with a hot ice-pick as described above, then thread a wire-core wick through. Fill the rest of the hole with hot wax and let it harden. Finally, dip the candle into a hot wax bath to add a shiny glaze. These can be made in many colors at Candlemas to celebrate Brigit, then burned at Ostara to celebrate the Earth's fertility.

Striped candles. If you want striped candles, melt several colors of wax in different pans. Pour an inch of one color into the mold, let it harden for 15–30 minutes, then pour in the next color, and so on. Have plenty of other activities to keep people busy in between, while the wax cools! You can tilt the mold in different directions for each pour, resulting in diagonal stripes.

Swirly-magickal candles. For misty, swirly, magickal-looking candles, pour in some clear or white wax, let it cool for just a minute or so, and then pour in a contrasting color. Keep alternating waxes, but never let the wax get cool enough to make defined layers; let the colors intermingle somewhat.

Ice candles. For really unusual, special candles, make ice candles. Pour ¼ inch of wax in the bottom of a quart-sized cardboard milk carton and stick a thin taper into the puddle. Hold it vertical for about 15 minutes as the wax cools. Then break up some ice into chunks smaller than ice cubes, and loosely fill the mold with the ice, around the taper. Pour the rest of the hot wax in over the ice. Use one color of wax, or, for a swirly effect, pour in two colors of wax (red and white, perhaps?).

After the candle has cooled a few minutes (it goes quickly because of the ice), set it upside down where the water can drain out as the ice finishes melting. The next day remove the mold and light your candle. It will have fascinating little caverns and crevices through which the light can shine.

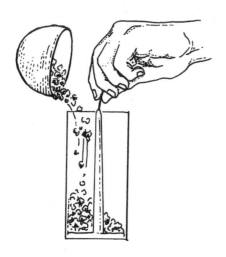 

Sand-cast candle. Get a bucket of sand, dampen the sand enough that it is moldable, and dig out the shape you want for your candle. This is one kind of candle that is usually poured right side up. You can put feet on it by poking with your fingers or a dowel rod at the bottom after the main body of the candle is shaped. And you can add textures, for example using a large

fork to create stripes in the sides. Consider making bumps in the mold with your fingers, and cutting them off after the candle cools. The cut places will glow like little jewels in the sand base. Go wild!

Do not spray your "mold" with silicone—the object is to have some of the sand stick to the wax. Add the wick, using a wick-holder and wire wicking, and pour in the wax.

Hotter wax with drier sand will cause a thicker shell of sand on the final candle; cool wax and wet sand will leave a light dusting of sand. The wax will shrink as it cools, so prick the center and add more wax until the candle is flat on top. When the wax has cooled, gently dig out the candle and brush off excess sand, dead fish, etc. Enjoy!

Berry candle. Begin with a simple pillar candle. Prepare a shallow bowl full of dried, cleaned berries. Holly berries, pyracanthus berries, and even rose hips work well. Hold the pillar candle by the wick and dip it into melted paraffin lightly colored to match the berries; again, don't use stearine. Then, quickly, while the wax is still warm, roll the candle in the berries, and press the berries into the wax. Let it cool, and repeat the process two or three times, until the whole surface of the candle is covered with berries.

Dip the whole thing twice more into the hot wax, letting the wax cool thoroughly between dippings. After the final wax coating, dip it very quickly into cool water to bring up a high gloss. You will have a festive, yummy-looking candle, but remember that it is not edible—keep it out of the reach of curious little people.

Pines-in-the-mist candles. You can create lovely candles by putting the decorations *inside*. For these, do not use stearine in the wax; stearine makes wax opaque and the object is to see into the candle. First cut snips of pine branches, holly with berries, ferns, and the like, and have them handy. For these candles it is very important to prepare your mold with silicone spray or an oil coating. Add wicking. Pour the hot melted wax into the mold, then pour almost all of it back out, creating a very thin layer of wax inside the mold.

Dip the snippets of evergreen into the pot of melted wax, and while they're still warm, shape them as you want. Then press them into the thin layer of wax on the inside of the mold, flattening them against the sides. Carefully pour cool wax (just above melting temperature) into the mold, rotating it to add a thin layer to the sides. Let this layer cool, then repeat once or twice. By this time, your snippets and the outer layers of wax have cooled enough that they won't lose their shape when the rest of the hot wax is poured in. Be sure the outer layers are really cool before you finally pour in the rest of the wax.

Finishing Your Candle

For decorated candles, let them cool longer than you would expect them to need, just to be sure the wax is as hard as it will get. Gently tap the mold and the candle should slide out. If it doesn't, try dropping it, open end down, onto a soft cloth on a hard counter or floor. If necessary, dip it for a *few* seconds into hot water. Or put it in the freezer for half an hour; the wax will contract and should come free. If you need a jackhammer or high explosives to get your candle out of the mold, you should use more silicone spray or peanut oil next time.

Scrape away any excess wax, and if your mold had a seam, carefully cut away the standing stripe on the side of the candle. Cut off extra wicking if you don't need it, but leave a couple of inches to hold if you plan to do any post-decorating dipping. Polish the final product with a plain nylon stocking.

Now you're ready to put your new candle in a beautiful holder, and use it to decorate your home or altar—or do some magick!

Candles in Magick

Candles have been used for centuries to perform spells or other works of magick. Candle magick evolved from the old lunar cults where torches were lighted to invoke the Moon Goddess. The lighted candle symbolizes the presence of the Moon Goddess who is the Enchantress, Mistress of Magick. All acts of magick performed in the glow of her flame are empowered by the momentum of the past.[1]

Choose or create your magickal candle in the correct color to symbolize the desired outcome (see chart, pp. 168–171), then anoint it with oil, and carve or decorate it. Next, magickally charge or energize the candle for its specific purpose, and finally burn it, usually while you recite a chant to get the magick moving. You can notch the candle, and allow it to burn down one notch each evening while you concentrate on the desired outcome. However, some spells require that the candle be allowed to burn all the way down in one sitting. (If you have pets, leave the burning candle in a room with the door closed and the animals outside!) In other spells, the candle may be forcefully snuffed in water, salt, or earth, or broken in two. In certain workings, two candles may be joined together to burn as one.

If more than two candles are being used, the candle in the center may represent the person doing the magick, or the person for whom the magick is being done—only with their permission, of course! Other candles may symbolize the desired outcome. The candles may be burned from the new moon to the full, or vice versa. During this process those on the outside are moved toward the center to attract what they symbolize (such as health or prosperity), or away from the center to banish something negative (such as illness or poverty).

Always keep a pair of candles of each basic color on hand, so you can do magick as needed. As long as the candles have not been consecrated to any specific purpose, they may all be kept together. Wrap them in paper, or keep the colors in separate boxes, so the colors do not come off on other candles.

You may want to dress and consecrate your candles in advance. It is traditional to bless candles at Imbolg or Candlemas, especially those to be used in magick, to remove any negative or irrelevant energy and replace it with positive. Then, to contain the energy, wrap each on, preferably in white linen or silk, tied with a cord or thread. Add a small tag, identifying the purpose to which each will be put.

Choosing Candle Colors

Standard colors associated with certain desired outcomes are listed in the chart on pages 168–171. However, choosing candle colors is a personal thing, just like any other magickal symbolism. For example, perhaps pink represents safety to me because my childhood room felt like a safe haven and the walls were pink. If you are doing a spell for yourself, use whatever color feels right for you.

If you are doing a spell with a group, using the standard colors may help the magick, as everyone can tune in to the shared meanings.

Herbs, Fragrances, Metals, and Stones

Candles are a great way to combine herb-lore, aromatherapy, and the languages of metals, stones, and symbols. Herbs can be added to candles either during their making, or as oils or washes later. Herbs are most commonly added to candles in the form of fragrant essential oils, which mix thoroughly with the wax, providing a constant delight as they burn.

Whole herbs inside the candle imbue the entire candle with their magickal properties, but in some cases can interfere with clean burning. They work best inside large-diameter candles, because the plant matter can be kept away from the wick. Use entire sprigs of fresh or dried herbs.

You can anoint candles with any essential oil, or any oil in which herbs have been steeped. Jojoba, almond, or other oils with little character of their own are good for absorbing the essence of fragrant herbs. Oil may be applied to a candle from base to tip, so the magick will rise to meet the flame, then combine with the smoke or heat and be on its way. Meditate on this to a simple, repetitive chant. Don't hurry; if it's worth doing, it's worth doing well!

Place metals and stones inside candles to imbue them with their properties. Cleanse the stones in salt water or sunlight first. Gold has very special properties, and can be easy to add to candles. Buy gold leaf at your crafts store and either line the mold with it before (carefully!) pouring the wax—it will crumple anyway—or apply it to the finished candle using plain white glue. You can apply the glue in patterns, and after it dries only the gold leaf stuck to the glue will adhere to the candle.

Symbols to Carve

Carving symbols on candles is as ancient as candle magick itself. The carving may be simple notches to mark how far the candle should burn each night of the spell; or it can be as complicated as a talismanic seal from a medieval grimoire.

When carving into a candle, first place it in a bowl of hot water for a moment to slightly soften the wax, or chips will flake off as you carve. Carve the candle with a hobby knife or dental tools. Once the design is carved, consider dipping the candle a few times into a contrasting color wax. More wax will collect in the carved spaces than on the remaining flat surfaces, making the design stand out. This also smooths the surface of the candle, creating a more polished surface.

Candle Safety

Finally, a few words to the wise. If you have small children or active pets, be very careful where you place your burning candles, and never leave a burning candle unattended. If you need to leave it burning for a magick spell, place the candle on a non-flammable surface, in the fireplace, or in a large bowl. Never place a candle near anything that can blow into the flame (those delicate gauze curtains, for instance), and always snuff the candle completely when you're done.

Enjoy your live flames during the Festival of Fire!

Candle Spell Colors, Herbs/Oils,

Purpose & Ruling Deities	Colors	Herbs, Oils, & Perfumes
BLESSING–Isis, Danu, Baldur, the Sun, Demeter	White, pink, green	Lavender, frankincense, rosemary, vanilla, myrrh
CALMING–Quan Yin, Isis, Baldur, the Sun, Brede, Gaea, Branwen, Lahkshmi	Light blue or light green, yellow	Chamomile, rose, gardenia, lavender, tuberose, sandalwood, frankincense
CLEAR OBSTACLES–Isis, Ganesh, The Norns, Saturn	White, violet	White rose, angelica, violet, vanillin
COURAGE–Athene, Mars, Tiw, Artemis, Thor Marduk, Hercules, Anat	Red, yellow	Cinnamon, dragon's blood, geranium, pine, honeysuckle
FERTILITY–Demeter, Pan, Frigg, Venus, Arianrhod, Gaea, Shiva, Bacchus	Bright green	Olive oil, mugwort, white rose
GROUNDING–Gaia, Uma, Demeter, Dagda, Cernunnos, Osiris, Innana, Hera, Pan	Brown, green, umber, dark gold	Dragon's blood, copal, piñon, cedar, mugwort, pine, olive oil, sage
HAPPINESS–Pan, the Sun, Baldur, Bast, Dionysis	Yellow, orange	Orange peel, cinnamon, carnation, basil
HEALING– Brede, Quan Yin, the Sun, Isis, Shiva, Apollo, the Dagda, Pan, Cernunnos, Lugh, Baldur, Hygeia, Minerva, Skadi	Rose, gold, green, red, purple, light blue	All-heal or herb particular to the ailment, rosemary, juniper, apricot, bergamot, carnation, orange blossom, thyme
HOUSE BLESSING–Thor, Jupiter, Gaia, Hera, Bast, Apollo, Demeter, Hestia	Light blue, white, brown	Myrrh, vanilla, juniper, pine needles, salt, narcissus
INITIATION–Isis, Hecate, Cerridwen, Ceres, Osiris, the Dagda, Thoth, Juno	White	Frankincense, myrrh, amber

Metals/Stones, Symbols, and Days

Metals and Stones	Symbols	Day of the Week
Rose quartz, diamond, ruby, sapphire, garnet		Saturday
Gold, pyrite, hematite, aquamarine, citrine, pearl, clear quartz, jade	Waves	Sunday
Clear quartz, garnet, fluorite, turquoise	X through symbol of obstacle	Saturday
Iron, ruby, garnet, aventurine, agate, citrine, bloodstone		Tuesday
Copper, moss agate, coral, Botswana agate	E, sprouting plant	Friday
Galena, hematite, agate, petrified wood, pyrite, citrine, granite, coral	Tree with roots	
Gold, copper, carnelian, citrine, turquoise	Smiley-face	Sunday
Gold, agate, emerald, sapphire, lapis lazuli, carnelian, clear quartz, turquoise, garnet, amber, bloodstone	Caduceus	Wednesday, Sunday
Tin, rose quartz, hematite, zircon, lodestone	House inside heart	Thursday, Saturday
Clear quartz, amethyst, opal, sapphire		Sunday, Monday

Candle Spell Colors, Herbs/Oils,

Purpose & Ruling Deities	Colors	Herbs, Oils, & Perfumes
LOVE–Brigit, Branwen, Frigg, Venus, Cupid, Eros, Aphrodite, Venus, Inanna, Isis, Selene, Krishna, Bast	Pink, Rose	Rose, amber, cinnamon, musk, lime, rosewood, patchouli, nutmeg, orange blossom
MENTAL FOCUS–Mercury, Odin, Janus, Brigit, Diana, Horus, Ganesh, Osiris	Royal blue, orange, yellow	Orange peel, lavender, civet, sandalwood, benzoin, clary sage, carnation, heather
MOTIVATION–Isis, Brigit, Baldur, the Sun, Apollo, Badb, Cerridwen, Freya	Yellow, red, purple	Lemon, ginger, marigold, chamomile, heliotrope, bayberry
PASSION–Circe, Frigg, Eros, Aphrodite, Mars, Venus, Parvati, Krishna, Ishtar, Dionysius, Lilith	Red, bright yellow Red and orange	Cinnamon, musk for sexual passion, violet, mint, dill, sandalwood, vanilla
PROSPERITY–Lahkshmi, Jupiter, Thor, the Sun, Mercury, Cernunnos, the Dagda, Vishnu, Inari	Green, gold, silver, orange	Rue, cedar, sage, nutmeg, blue lilac, clove, amber oil, almond oil, benzoin, lemon balm, cinnamon
PROTECTION–Isis, Thor, The Norns, Indra, Hecate	Royal blue, white, violet	Lavender, rosemary, pepper, brimstone, vanilla
PSYCHIC SKILLS–Brigit, Odin, Mercury, the Moon, the Morrigan, Osiris, Isis	Lavender, violet, silver, dark blue	Mustard, frankincense, peony, hyacinth, acacia
SAFE TRAVEL–Hermes, The Norns, Lugh, Jupiter, Janus, Artemis, Ganesh	Yellow	Comfrey root, rosemary, caraway, lavender, juniper
SELF-CONTROL–Anubis, Jupiter, Odin, Ganesh, Thoth, Maat, Danu, Isis	Purple	Lavender, dill
TRANSFORMATION–Isis, Freya, the Moon, Hecate, Kephera, Janus, Brigit	Orange	Copal, camphor, jasmine, heather, myrtle, mugwort, lotus, magnolia

Metals/Stones, Symbols, and Days

Metals and Stones	Symbols	Day of the Week
Copper, rose quartz, lapis lazuli, lodestone, sapphire, emerald, diamond, aquamarine	Hearts, interlocked rings	Friday
Amethyst, moonstone, clear quartz, garnet, citrine		Monday
Gold, fluorite, agate, aventurine, garnet, bloodstone	The words: "I CAN DO IT!"	Sunday
Copper, Mexican fire agate, garnet	The word "YES", exclamation points	Tuesday, Friday
Gold, sunstone, zircon, Agate, blue aventurine	Dollar Signs, cornucopia	Thursday, Sunday
Hematite, carnelian, bloodstone, agate	Triangle	Saturday
Lapis lazuli, clear quartz, amethyst		Monday or Wednesday
Malachite—land, aquamarine—water, moonstone—night		Saturday
Amethyst, citrine, agate, aventurine		Wednesday
Copper, amethyst, emerald	Arrow	Monday

Notes

1. Grimassi, *Encyclopedia of Wicca and Witchcraft*, p. 57.

Preparing the Feast:
Ancient and
Modern Dishes

What is a festival without a feast? In keeping with an end-of-winter celebration honoring an ancient Irish goddess and saint, we will focus mostly
on foods that would have been available in old Ireland in late winter.
Foods for the celebration were left over from the previous harvest and
kept edible mostly by smoking, drying, or storing in a cool, dark root cellar. The people would have had turnips, carrots, and lots of onions, leeks,
and garlic. They stored cabbages and beets, radishes, lentils, dried peas
(for lots of pease porridge), and beans of many kinds. The only fresh
green vegetable was watercress surviving in a year-round stream. Their
main vegetable was the ubiquitous turnip.

The primary staple was corn, but not the maize that we call corn in
America. In old Europe, "corn" meant the most prevalent grain grown in
the area: wheat in England; oats or barley in Scotland and Ireland; and
wheat, barley, and rye on the Continent. These grains were made into

porridge, flatcakes, and heavy breads often used as trenchers, or plates, under servings of stew that moistened them enough to eat.

Meat was sparse, yet of a greater variety than most of us eat today. There was smoked, salted, or spiced red meat (ham, bacon, and sausage) from the previous Samhain's butchering, plus rabbit, venison, quail, partridge, and other wild game. Villagers raised chickens, ducks, and geese. Fresh, smoked, and salted fish of all kinds were staples, and eels were a special delicacy. The occasional Imbolc lamb did not survive, and they'd eat stringy old mutton from sheep that had outlived their wool, or an occasional cow too old to give milk.

To flavor their slightly rancid meat and months-old vegetables, almost everyone had an herb garden and dried the herbs—especially dill, fennel, sage, and probably parsley. Dried mushrooms were common. Of spices, only the trade in pepper seems to have survived the fall of the Roman Empire, and then only in limited quantities—so it was used sparingly; a pound was worth more than two weeks' wages! They had no white sugar, either, so no preserves as we know them. The main sweetener was honey.

Much protein came from non-meat sources: dried peas and beans; eggs of all kinds; milk from goats, sheep, or cows; and many kinds of cheeses.

Fruits included the native apples, pears, blackberries, and plums. The apples could have been stored in a cold cellar, but all the rest would have been dried for winter storage. Cherries may have been brought to England by Roman legionnaires, spitting out the pits of dried cherries along the roads as they marched; the seedlings were brought to Ireland by traders. There were English walnuts and hazelnuts—but no almonds, chestnuts, black walnuts, pecans, cashews, peanuts, or Brazil nuts, all from the New World or Far East.

To wash it all down, the people had ale, darker and more bitter than beer; but no beer made with hops until after the Crusades. They also drank cider and mead, and apple, cherry, blackberry, plum, and pear wines, as well as wines made from vegetables—including, again, the turnip! Although grape wine was known to the Celts in France, the British did not see much of it until after the Crusades.

Diet varied according to class. Until as late as the sixteenth century, the poor ate mostly porridge or dark bread with ale; then the potato gradually became their staple starch, replacing the bitter turnip. Occasionally they tasted a little meat or fish, and milk if they were rich enough to own a cow. But the cauldron over the fire was rarely empty, with fresh meat or fish added to the remains of whatever had gone before, along with water and grain. Every evening this was heated for dinner, and after dinner it was left to cool until morning. Hence the nursery rhyme, "Pease porridge hot, pease porridge cold, pease porridge in the pot, nine days old." Or nine months old. . . . The nobility ate better, but bread and ale were still their staples. Much more meat made it to their tables, but in winter they saw no more vegetables than the poor.

Breakfast for everyone was ale, bread, cheese, and meat or fish—in short, the same as any other meal. A hearty English breakfast today still resembles the ancient breakfast much more than the caffeine, white flour, and sugar concoctions of the United States and the Continent. Consider starting your celebration of Brigit's day the way she would have: with dark bread or thick porridge, a piece of leftover meat, and perhaps a small mug of ale.

The Bright Side of the Crusades

The returning Crusaders brought many tasty things back to Britain: expensive exotics such as lemons and oranges, cinnamon, cloves, ginger, nutmeg, dried figs and dates, and cuttings of eastern peach and apricot trees and currant bushes. While the lemons and oranges did not last into the winter, the spices did, and in the wealthy houses were used liberally to cover the taste of meat that wasn't surviving well.

The peasantry still had no money to buy spices, but the growing merchant middle class could afford some luxuries; and spices were a favorite commodity, for the meat on the merchants' tables was no more fresh than that of the lord and lady in the big house. Little did they know that not only do cinnamon and clove taste good, but they have antiseptic properties in the intestines and probably saved no few lives.

In time, the almond and the chestnut were introduced. Herbs became more varied and widely used, especially Mediterranean herbs like rosemary, thyme, oregano, marjoram, coriander, basil, and mint. But one of the greatest gifts the Crusaders brought back was wine made from grapes, which added a whole new flavor to cooking as well as drinking.

The Irish Thank Columbus for the Potato

After Columbus reached the New World and other explorers opened the great trading routes to the East, the foods of the whole world became available to the rich. From America came tomatoes, peppers, maize, turkey, pumpkins, and potatoes (there were no potatoes in Ireland until the sixteenth century). The big, round, orange fruits we call pumpkins are native to the Americas; Europeans who wanted to carve jack-o-lanterns used turnips. Soon there were raspberries, strawberries, and blueberries—and perhaps the Americas' greatest gift, chocolate! From the East came tea, coffee, and hops for beer.

Cultivated yeast became a necessity, baking soda was discovered as a leavening, and baking powder was invented in 1856. In short, Europe had everything we've got available today.

As for the poor, grain gave way in large part to the potato. The basic necessities were summed up in the old folk saying, "A smoky cabin, a handful of spuds, and a flea-filled bed." The diet of the poor remained long on starch, short on meat, and woefully short of vegetables. They did get a little white sugar, a little tea, yeast for baking, and hops for beer.

You may wonder what all this has to do with your modern festivities. After all, today we have access to all these wonderful foods, so why not use them? There's no reason not to, unless you want to try to understand what the end of winter was like for our ancestors, at least for one meal. (Turn off your heating and lights and gather around the fireplace, but remember the Irish proverb: "The well-filled belly has little understanding of the empty." We'll never really know what it was like).

We've gathered together recipes for the foods the early Irish would have had for their Brigit's feasts, a few recipes appropriate to the season from after the Crusades, and a few more using post-Columbus or modern ingredients. Each recipe is marked for its time period, so you can easily put together feasts true to the ancients, the late Middle Ages, or modern Irish, as you please. These codes will help you plan your feast:

A: Ancient

PCR: Post-Crusades

PCOL: Post-Columbus

V: Vegetarian, or easily adapted

Note: "Salt and pepper to taste" is not authentically Ancient, but our tastebuds are so accustomed to them that we've used them here.

A Note to Vegetarians

While few Europeans were vegetarian by choice until the last half of the twentieth century, many people are today. Many of these recipes can be adapted for vegetarians by the simple expedient of leaving out the meat, and substituting vegetable stock for chicken or beef stock. Often these recipes originated as their vegetarian cousins, and a family felt themselves lucky when the meat was available to add.

So, with a hearty breakfast under our belts, here we go, back into the mists of time when a goddess walked the earth—and needed something to eat, just like the rest of us!

Breads and Grain Dishes

The earliest breads were flatbreads, essentially porridges that had been cooked on a hot rock or griddle until stiff. The discovery of leavening may have been an accident: a bakery next to a brewhouse getting a whiff of yeast through a window, or perhaps a bit of fermenting dough being thrown into the next batch of bread, "to see what happens." Voilà, sourdough! As Adrian Bailey says in *The Blessings of Bread* (p. 185):

> Practically anything will make a starter, anything, that is, having the qualities to ferment. You can make a starter out of flour and milk, or flour and water; rye flour plus water and a slice of onion; flour, water, sugar, and hops; corn meal, beer, and tea leaves; old shoes; hot water and sugar mixed with the pulp of old books about bread and magazines devoted to food and wine; water, hops, a slice of onion, a large slice of cheesecake and a finely shredded copy of the Sunday edition of the *New York Times*.

Most of these were not known to old Ireland, but the concept is there. Bread is easy. Flour. Water. Leavening. Knead. Bake. All the rest is window dressing and flavoring and fun.

> *Rye bread will do you good*
> *Barley bread will do you no harm*
> *Wheaten bread will sweeten your blood*
> *Oaten bread will strengthen your arm.*

> —Old Irish Proverb

The ancient breads were heavy, often sour, and made good plates, or trenchers, but were difficult to eat by themselves without being dipped in soup or broth. To suit modern tastes, we're skipping ahead to modern breads made with cultivated yeast, soda, and baking powder, beginning with some now-traditional Irish variations.

Oatmeal Porridge, Barley Porridge, Millet Porridge . . . (A, V)

Use wheat, rye, barley, oats, millet, or any combination. See Millet and Mushrooms for millet-rinsing instructions.)

Method one: cover whole grains with milk, let sit for 12 hours, heat to boiling, serve with honey.

Method two: stir ground grain into warming milk until just before boiling, remove from heat and let it sit for five minutes (or simmer for three). Serve with a splash of heavy cream, and honey or dried fruit.

Flummery (A, V)

Cover oats with water and let sit for 36 hours, changing water at least every 12 hours. Pour off final water. Heat, stirring constantly, until it thickens; and serve with milk or heavy cream and honey or dried fruit, or with beer and cheese.

Irish Potato Bread (PCOL, V)

Preheat oven to 450 degrees

To	1	cup mashed potatoes leftover from last night
Add, and mix well	1	teaspoon salt
	2	tablespoons melted butter
Then add	½	cup white flour
to make workable dough, adding more flour if needed		

Roll out ½-inch-thick circle, transfer to baking sheet, and cut into 6 or 8 wedges, but don't separate. Bake in 450 degree oven until golden brown. Or cook on griddle, turning once so they are golden brown on both sides.

Serve with butter. Serves 1–8, depending on appetites.

Brede's Braid Bread (PCOL, V)

In large bowl, combine   2¼   cups white flour

1   tablespoon salt

2   tablespoons sugar

2   packages dry yeast

Add, and beat by hand or   ¼   cup butter, softened or melted

in mixer for 2 minutes, until   2   eggs, slightly beaten

all ingredients are combined   2¼   cups very warm, *not hot*, water

(120–130 degrees)

Then add   1   cup white flour

Beat at high speed for 2 minutes (or if making by hand, knead it more later). Divide equally into three bowls. (This is most accurately done by weight with a kitchen scale, but by eye and intuition works, too.)

In first bowl add and beat in   2   tablespoons molasses

1¼   cups whole wheat flour

In second bowl add, beat in   1¼   cups yellow cornmeal

In third bowl add, beat in   1¼   cups white flour

Knead each batter on slightly floured board (use whole wheat flour, cornmeal, or white flour on board), about 5 minutes if you've been beating the dough in a mixer, about 10 minutes if you've been mixing by hand. Dough should be smooth and elastic, bouncing back when poked. Grease all three bowls, place doughs in them, cover with damp cloths, and let rise in warm place (oven with pilot light works well) until doubled, about an hour. Punch down. On lightly floured board, divide each dough in half, roll each half into a rope about 15 inches long. Braid together a white, a corn, and a whole wheat rope. (It's easiest if you start in the middle, go to one end, and turn the braid around to finish the other end.) Tuck ends under, and repeat with three remaining ropes. Place in greased 9 by 4-inch loaf pans. Cover with damp cloth over waxed paper, let rise again until doubled, about an hour.

Heat oven to 350 degrees. Bake 25–30 minutes, until cornmeal braid is light brown on the top.

Baste with   2   tablespoons melted butter

Return to oven for 10 more minutes. Loaf should sound hollow when tapped.

Remove from oven, remove from pans onto wire racks, cover with damp cloth and let cool at least half an hour before cutting (I know, the waiting is agony).

Serve with lots of butter. Excellent toasted the next morning if there's any left, serve with butter and apple butter or jam. Makes 2 loaves. Double the recipe and you might have some left for tomorrow! Variation: Make entire batch one grain. Our favorite is all cornmeal, and is superb toasted!

Oatcakes (PCOL, V)

Preheat oven to 350 degrees

In blender, pulverize	1	cup regular oatmeal, place in bowl
Add	¼	teaspoon baking powder
	½	teaspoon salt
	1	tablespoon butter, melted
Stir and add slowly	2–3	tablespoons hot water
to make smooth, firm paste		
On board, sprinkle	¼	cup oatmeal flakes

Roll ball on oatmeal until it is a circle about 8 inches wide and ⅛ inch thick. Cut into 8 wedges.

On baking sheet, sprinkle   ¼   cup oatmeal flakes

Place wedges on oatmeal and bake for about 15 minutes, until light brown. Open oven door, but leave wedges in oven until firm and crisp.

Serve with cheese, honey, or jam.

Millet and Mushrooms (A, V)

Millet is an ancient, hardy grain. It grows almost anywhere, stores well, and cooks quickly because of its small size. It was used in the Swiss lake settlements as early as about 2800 B.C.E., but did not become widespread on the European continent until about 100 B.C.E. Before cooking, be sure to rinse it in a sieve, stirring constantly for about 5 minutes, to remove the bitter outer husks.

In saucepan, melt	2	tablespoons butter
Add	1	clove garlic, minced
	1	medium onion, chopped

Cook until onion is browned, stirring frequently.

Add	1	cup rinsed millet
	2	cups broth (beef, chicken or vegetable)
	2	cups boiling water

Stir, bring back to boil, cover and keep on a high simmer for 25–30 minutes. Keep adding water as needed until all the millet has expanded and popped its husk. After that, reduce heat and simmer until all the water is absorbed. Meanwhile,

Melt	1	tablespoon butter
Sauté	1	cup large, tasty mushrooms, diced small

For portabella, oyster, morel . . . try your specialty market. For authenticity, stay away from the definitely Asian mushrooms, like shiitake.

Combine sautéed mushrooms with millet.

Add	Salt and pepper to taste

Top with a pat of butter. Serves 6.

Something to Go with Bread

Dipping Dinner (A, V)

In saucepan, stir together, and cook until onion is tender

¼ cup finely chopped onions (green onions if you have any left from last autumn's harvest)

1 clove garlic, minced or well crushed

1 tablespoon butter

Stir in, and simmer 5 min.
Then stir in

1 cup beer or ale

1 cup shredded Cheddar cheese

1 cup shredded sharp Cheddar cheese

1 teaspoon arrowroot powder (optional, helps keep it from clumping)

1 cup cream cheese

Serve with hearty bread "fingers," carrot sticks, turnip sticks, or breadsticks. Serves 6.

Fried Leeks and Bacon (A)

In water to cover, boil, then strain off liquid

1 side bacon

In deep skillet, heat
Add

2 tablespoons oil

Bacon

1 pound leeks, chopped

1 medium onion

Salt and pepper to taste

Cover and simmer for 25 minutes. Serve hot on slabs of hearty bread. Serves 4.

Welsh Rarebit (PCR, V)

The rarebit itself is just a sauce. It's what you serve the sauce over that determines the extent of the feast.

In large saucepan, melt	2	tablespoons butter
Whisk in	3	tablespoons whole wheat flour
	1	teaspoon dry mustard

Cook about 5 minutes, whisking constantly.

Stir in, and cook until thick, about 10 minutes, whisking constantly	1½	cups ale or beer, stout; or porter for more flavor
Then stir in	1	pound Cheddar cheese, grated A grinding of black pepper

Cook another 10 minutes over very low heat, stirring occasionally.

Serve over	Toasted bread, sprinkled with apples, mushrooms, sliced onions, other vegetables, or English walnuts.

Post-Columbus, serve over English muffins, with sliced tomatoes. Serves 4–6.

Late Winter Soups

"All That's Left is Potatoes and Leeks" Soup (A, V)

In large pot, melt	2	tablespoons butter
Add, and warm, stirring constantly	2	cups of potato slices (¼-inch thick), browned in frying pan
Add	3	cups beef, chicken, rabbit, or vegetable stock
		Salt and pepper to taste
	6	sliced leeks

Simmer for 15 minutes. Reduce heat.

| Add | ½ cup warmed heavy cream |

Sprinkle with parsley, serve immediately. Serves 6.

For a variation, make "All That's Left is Oatmeal and Leeks" Soup, but start with ¼ cup oatmeal instead of the potato slices.

Irish Stew (PCOL)

For Ancient Stew, substitute 1 cup barley pearls for potatoes. Do not boil this, rather allow it to gently "walk," or simmer.

Remove fat from, and dice	2	pounds mutton
Slice thinly	1	potato or ⅔ cup barley
Chop	1	onion

Place these in large stew pot, meat on the bottom, and

Add	2	cups water

Bring to near boil, skim, cover, and simmer for an hour.

Add, and simmer one more hour	1	pound potatoes, left whole if small, or cut in half (or 2 cups barley)
	5	medium onions, cut in half
	½	pound carrots, peeled and cut in 2-inch pieces
		Salt and pepper to taste
		Water to 12 cups

Serves at least 12.

Guinness Stew (PCOL)

Brigit was a beer girl—she would have loved this!

Remove excess fat from	1	pound round steak, cubed
In large stew pot, heat	2	tablespoons oil

Fry meat in oil until brown; remove from pot. Keep covered in dish.

Add to remaining oil	3	medium onions, sliced
	4	carrots, peeled and sliced
	4	stalks of celery, sliced across the rib
	6	potatoes, cut lengthwise in half and sliced

Fry until onions are limp, don't brown. Return meat to pan.

Add, gently sprinkling, and cook one minute, stirring	2	tablespoon flour
Gradually add	1	pint Guinness stout
Bring to boil, add	1	bouquet garni
		Salt and pepper to taste

Cover, place in oven for 2 hours at 400 degrees. Remove bouquet garni and serve with hearty bread (and more Guinness!) Serves 8–12.

One-Pot Meals

Corned Beef and Cabbage (A)

The beef available to the ancients was less than tender. "Corning," named for the corn-sized (grain-sized) rough salt granules used in the curing, allowed beef slaughtered at Samhain to last into the cold of winter without spoiling, and tenderized it, too. If you want to do it from scratch, see "Corned Beef" in The Joy of Cooking. It's easy, but takes about three weeks. Or, of course, you could go out and buy a nice brisket that's already corned.

Take your brisket and cover with boiling water in medium or BIG pot, depending on what you plan to add, and how many people you plan to feed. (Hint: today, as in ancient times, parsnips are cheap.)

Add	1	onion (studded with 4 to 6 whole cloves, post-Crusades version)
	1	bay leaf (post-Crusades, probably)
	6–8	peppercorns (or more if you love pepper)

Simmer about one hour per pound. During the cooking, add any or all of the following:

30 minutes before serving	Peeled and quartered parsnips, carrots, or turnips (post-Columbus: peeled, quartered potatoes!)
15 minutes before serving	Onions, peeled and quartered Cabbage, quartered, red or green
10 minutes before serving	Leeks, sliced

Serve with horseradish, mustard, or just plain salt and pepper.

Bubble and Squeak (PCOL, V)

This is named for the noises it makes while cooking. (The vegetarian version—without ham or bacon—is good, too; be sure to add salt.)

Boil and mash	2	cups potatoes
	2	cups turnips
Chop and blanch	2	cups cabbage, add to potatoes and turnips
Add	1	large onion, chopped coarsely
	1–2	cloves garlic, chopped
	1	cup cooked, diced ham
	4	cooked bacon slices (reserve the drippings)
		Salt, pepper, sage, tarragon, and thyme to taste

Heat bacon drippings (or 2 tablespoons butter) on griddle or large frying pan, add mixture to form a large, flat cake, and cook over medium heat. Serve in large wedges with beer, stout, or ale. Serves 6–8, depending on appetites.

Colcannon (PCOL, V)

Cut into 4 pieces   1   large head cabbage

Reserve outer leaves, wash it all thoroughly to remove sand. Chop remaining cabbage finely.

Peel, and cut into ½-inch slices   2   medium parsnips
                                    3   medium onions
                              10   medium potatoes (with skins)

Layer vegetables in saucepan: potatoes, then parsnips, onions, and cabbage.

Season with   Salt and pepper to taste
Repeat layers and seasoning
Add   1   pint water
Cover with   Cabbage outer leaves

Bring to boil, cover, and simmer until vegetables are soft, about 30 minutes. Strain off excess water, remove top leaves, and mash the rest together.

Add   ½   cup butter, stir into mash.

Place outer leaves on plates, spoon mash onto them, serve with more butter.
   Serves 8–12.

Amber's variation:

Layer mashed white potatoes, cabbage, mashed sweet potatoes, onions, mushrooms, and Cheddar cheese. Repeat. Do not mix; serve with layers intact, like lasagna. Add green chiles cut into strips (remove seeds) for a zing!

Here, Fishy, Fishy, Fishy!

Fish was popular—all of the British Isles were surrounded by fish-full seas and riddled with fish-full rivers, and anyone could catch one.

Fried Fish Fillets (A)

Wash and pat dry	Herring, halibut, sole, flounder, trout, or salmon fillets
Dredge in	Whole wheat flour
Then	Egg, slightly beaten
And finally	Oatmeal or oat flour
Brown on both sides in	Butter
Sprinkle lightly with	Salt and pepper when done.

A Trout in the Pan Is Better Than a Salmon in the Sea (PCR)

A trout in the pan . . . A salmon in the sea—Old Irish Proverb. Herbs and vinegar would be pre-Crusades; add spices and lemon for a post-Crusades version.

Mix together any combination of
Salt and pepper
Grated nutmeg, cloves
Rosemary, sprig of
Tarragon (a tiny bit, it's strong!)
Sage, marjoram, thyme, etc.

Go through your spice rack, and choose a different combination each time . . . very few combinations don't work.

Wash and pat dry   Salmon is best, or trout, halibut, bluefish, etc.

Rub with spices, place in buttered baking dish.

Pour on   4   tablespoons butter, melted, mixed with
           2   teaspoons apple cider vinegar or lemon juice

Bake 20 minutes per pound, basting frequently with butter and vinegar/lemon.

Sous'd Mackerel (PCR)

Preheat oven to 325 degrees
Butter a shallow oven dish.

Wash and dry	3	one-pound mackerels, eviscerated, no heads, leave the tails
Place in oven dish, with	1	medium onion, cut into ¼-inch rings
On top of fish, add	1	more onion, cut in rings
	¼	cup parsley, finely chopped
	⅛	teaspoon thyme, ground
	12	whole black peppercorns
Beside fish, add	2	small bay leaves
	1	cup white wine vinegar or white wine
	1	cup cold water
	2	tablespoons fresh lemon juice

Bring to a boil on top of stove, place in oven. Bake for 15 minutes until fish is firm, basting two or three times. Remove from oven, let cool, cover, and refrigerate for at least 6 hours. To serve, do not cut through spine. First serve top side of fish, down to bones, remove backbone, then serve lower side of fish. Serves 6.

Sauce

Mushroom~Dill Wine Sauce for Fish, Meat, Vegetables, or Grains (PCR, V)

In small bowl, whisk, set aside	1	tablespoon flour
	1	tablespoon water
In saucepan, combine	⅓	cup chicken or vegetable stock
	½–¾	pound mushrooms, cleaned and sliced thin
	3	shallots, peeled and sliced

Cover, simmer over low heat until mushrooms turn dark, about 8 minutes.

Add and simmer uncovered for 10 minutes	1¼	cups dry white wine
Add and whisk		Flour mixture
Add	1½	tablespoons fresh or
	¾	tablespoon dried dill

Stir constantly for about a minute. Let sit while you broil or grill your meat or fish, or steam your vegetables, then stir again, and pour over meat, fish, or vegetables. Serves 6.

From Forest and Farm

Honey-Apple Chicken
or Game Hen or Rabbit (A)

Until the twelfth century, the Gauls, and probably the Britons, roasted their meat on a spit rather than baking or broiling it in an oven. This recipe would have been used for spit-roasting, with a pot of lard next to the spit for basting.

Peel, core, and dice	1	apple (dried, for authenticity)
Chop coarsely	1	onion
Toss apple and onion with	1	tablespoon of salt
	1	teaspoon of pepper (not "A", but tasty)
Stuff into	1	chicken, 4 to 6 game hens, or place in roasting pan around pheasant, rabbit, beef, etc.
Melt together	4	tablespoons butter
	4	tablespoons honey
Baste meat with		Honey-butter (about 2 tablespoons each)

Roast (depending on quantity and kind of meat) about 1½ hours at about 325 degrees, basting halfway through. Cover for moist meat, uncovering for last 15 minutes to brown.

Oimelc Ham (A)

Mix in small bowl	¼	cup honey
	3	tablespoons powdered mustard
	1	cup heavy cream
Place in casserole	1	pound diced, cooked ham
and mix to coat with	2	turnips or parsnips
honey mixture	1	onion, or 3 leeks, diced

Cover and bake at 325 degrees for 40 minutes. (Or simmer in large skillet for 20 minutes, or until vegetables are done.) Serves 4–6.

Roast Rabbit (A)

Rinse	1	whole, skinned rabbit.
Melt	¼	cup butter
Add	¼	onion, chopped, sauté until golden
Mix with	3	cups breadcrumbs (whole wheat or oat)
	1–2	teaspoon dried sage
	1	teaspoon salt
	¼	teaspoon pepper
	1	slightly beaten egg to moisten

Stuff rabbit, sew together the opening, cut ends off hind legs, bring together with forelegs toward head and skewer in place. Lightly slash the flesh at the shoulder joints.

Over back of rabbit, drape   2   strips bacon

Place in baking dish, bake at 325 degrees for 1½ hours. Bake an additional 15 minutes if needed. Rabbit is done when, like chicken, there is no red showing when meat is cut to the bone. Serves 4.

Roast Lamb (A)

Preheat oven to 450 degrees

Wash and pat dry	4–5	pound cushion shoulder of lamb
Rub with		Garlic clove, cut
		Salt and pepper, lightly

Place roast into oven, uncovered on a rack over a roasting pan.

Reduce heat to 325 degrees and cook for about 30 minutes per pound. For rarer meat, internal temperature should reach 160–165 degrees; for well-done, 175–180 degrees.

Serve with mint jelly or apricot jam (post-Crusades), or with a gravy made from the drippings. Serves 8.

Forest Bounty (A)

In skillet, melt	2	tablespoons butter
Add	1	clove garlic, minced

Cook 1 minute or until beginning to brown but not burn, stirring constantly.

Add	1	pound ground venison

Cook until browned, drain off liquid (save it as soup stock).

Add	8	portabello mushrooms, cut in chunks (use dried, for authenticity, draining liquid after cooking these)

Cook until mushrooms are beginning to shrink and brown, stirring occasionally.

Add, and cook 5 minutes	1	tablespoon dried parsley
	1	teaspoon dried thyme, chopped
	2	teaspoons salt
	½	teaspoon ground black pepper
Serve over		Coarse dark bread, thickly sliced
Top with		Goat cheese, crumbled

Serves 6–8. Venison is very rich—small servings go a long way.

Basic Late Winter Meat Recipe (PCR)

Like the earlier Honey-Apple Chicken recipe, this can be used with almost any meat, but is especially good for poultry. The wine and stock would also serve to reconstitute tough dried meat, tenderizing as well as flavoring it.

Brown meat in butter, add

½ cup wine, usually white for poultry and red for red meats

1 cup chicken, beef, or vegetable broth

¼ teaspoon each salt, cinnamon, and cloves
Pinch of pepper

½ onion, chopped coarsely

Cover and let simmer for about 30 minutes.

Make a simple gravy from the broth (remove onion pieces first, for a smooth gravy) by whisking a tablespoon or two of flour into the broth after removing the meat. Pour over meat in serving dish, and serve with dark bread and the rest of the wine. Serves 4–6.

Vegetables

Stewed Seagreen (A, V)

This was a common vegetable for those living along the seacoast. It is among the most nutritious foods on the planet, supplying all required minerals, lots of vitamins, especially B_{12} and A. It is high in protein, and of course, iodine. Gathered in summer, it was dried for winter use.

Rinse well	Dried dulse or other seagreen (buy at your health food store)
Add	Milk or broth to cover generously
	Salt and pepper to taste

Simmer, covered, 1–3 hours, until tender. Serve with butter or sour cream.

Sunshine in Winter (A, V)

Alone, turnips have a slightly bitter aftertaste. Add something sweeter like apples, pears, carrots, or honey to decrease the bitterness.

Peel and slice	½	pound carrots
	1½	pounds turnips or parsnips

Boil separately in lightly salted water. Strain each, mash or purée together.

Add	Butter, salt, and pepper to taste

Serves 4.

Simple Pickles Made Last Summer (A, V)

In the summer, into sterilized, dry jars, stuff small cucumbers, cauliflower, onions, leeks, radishes, carrots, etc. Cover with apple cider vinegar. Add pepper, sage, tarragon, fennel seeds, etc., in various combinations. Cap with tight-fitting lids. Allow to sit in the dark for at least 4 months before eating. The vinegar may be re-used.

And Something Sweet

Stuffed Pancakes (A, V)

Make a whole-wheat pancake batter, using only salt and egg as leavening (no soda or baking powder!) and add diced apples or dried fruit, raisins, nuts, some precious cinnamon (post-Crusades), and a dollop of honey. Cook until puffy, serve hot with more honey. Serves about 6, depending on how much they've had for dinner beforehand.

The Best Scones (PCOL, V)

These scones are light and fluffy, and will melt in your mouth.

Preheat oven to 400 degrees

In bowl, mix	2	cups flour
	3	teaspoon baking powder
	½	teaspoon salt
	2	tablespoons sugar
Cut in	¼	cup softened butter
Mix in	¾	cup milk
	1	beaten egg

On a floured board, roll out to 1-inch thick circle, transfer to baking sheet. Cut with long knife to make 6 or 8 wedges but don't separate. Bake for 25 minutes.

Makes 6 or 8 scones; serves two because you can't stop eating them!

Serve with clotted cream (Devon cream in specialty foods store) and jam, or almost-whipped cream and jam, or this near-clotted cream:

In blender, whip together	1	cup sour cream
	1	teaspoon brown sugar
	1	teaspoon vanilla

Brigit's Cross Cookies (PCOL, V)

Also known as pinwheel cookies, variations on this theme can be found on the Internet from Good Housekeeping to AOL Food. We like them because they are creamy and crunchy.

Preheat oven to 350 degrees

With hand mixer, cream	½	cup butter
	3	ounces cream cheese
	1	cup sugar
Add, beating on low	1	egg, well beaten
	2	tablespoons buttermilk or yogurt
	1	cup flour, added slowly
	½	teaspoon baking powder
	½	teaspoon salt
	1	teaspoon vanilla extract
Add, using strong spoon	1	more cup flour

Divide dough in half, make into two ½-inch-thick discs, wrap in plastic, and chill until firm, 1–2 hours.

For filling, soften	3	ounces cream cheese
With a strong spoon, add	¾	cup sweetened coconut
	⅓	cup white chocolate chips
	¼	cup chopped macadamia nuts or almonds

Use parchment paper or grease 3 baking sheets.

On a lightly floured surface, roll one disc into an 8 by 13-inch rectangle about ⅛-inch thick. Using pizza cutter, pastry wheel, or plain old knife, cut into fifteen 2½-inch squares, transfer to baking sheets, about 1½ inch apart. Place 1 teaspoon filling (flat, not heaping) in center of each. Cut 1-inch diagonals in from corners toward filling. Fold every other corner in to center end of opposite cut, over filling, glue together with a drop of water if needed.

For glaze, use	2	tablespoons milk

Using pastry brush (or put milk into a clean squirt bottle), lightly dampen tops of pinwheels.

Sprinkle with   Granulated sugar
                       Colored sugar, red (lightly!)

Bake for about 12 minutes, until pastry is golden and puffed. While first batch is baking, prepare second batch. Cool on baking sheets for 5 minutes before transferring the finished cookies to rack to cool. Bake second batch. Makes 30 cookies.

Fire and Snow Trifle (PCOL, V)

If you have a favorite custard recipe, use it. If not, try one of the custard recipes in The Joy of Cooking, *or this one, or the one on the side of a package of Rennet, available in the baking/pudding area of your food store.*

The Custard

Custards can be very fussy, depending on altitude, relative humidity, and other imponderable factors. Whatever you do, don't let the steam condense into the custard, or it will be too watery. Make the custard the day before so you can try another version if it doesn't work.

In saucepan, whisk together	½	cup milk
	4	teaspoons cornstarch, until cornstarch is dissolved
Add, stirring constantly	2½	cups milk
	2	tablespoons sugar

Bring to boil, reduce heat.

In small bowl, whisk	3	egg yolks
Stir in	¼	cup of milk mixture

Return egg to main milk mixture, whisking constantly. Bring to boil again, boil for 1 minute, stirring constantly. Remove pan from heat.

Add	1	teaspoon vanilla extract

Keep stirring until custard no longer steams. Place in refrigerator, uncovered, to chill. Cool 1 hour or until firm. (If it hasn't set in 2 hours, it's not going to—try another recipe.)

Now you're ready to assemble the Trifle itself.

The Trifle

Strawberries may be substituted for raspberries.

Cut into 1-inch-thick slices	12	ounce pound cake
Spread with	4	tablespoons raspberry jam
In glass trifle bowl, place	3	slices of cake, jam side up
Add	½	cup blanched, slivered, or halved almonds
	½	cup dry sherry
	¼	cup brandy
Scatter over top	1	cup fresh raspberries
		or one 10-ounce bag frozen
Set aside	10	perfect raspberries, fresh or frozen
Spread	½	cooled custard over cake
Cut		Remaining cake into 1-inch cubes
Add		Cake cubes
Sprinkle over custard	½	cup almonds
	½	cup sherry
	¼	cup brandy
		Remaining ½ custard
Scatter over top	1	cup fresh or frozen raspberries
Whip	1	cup whipping cream
Add, beat until stiff	1	tablespoon confectioners' sugar

Spread the whipped cream over top, garnish with reserved raspberries.
Serve at once. Serves 8 generously.

Strawberry Cream (PCOL, V)

Strawberries are ripe in Ireland from early June to late August. Heavenly! Thank the Lady for refrigeration and Chilean strawberries.

In blender, whip	1	pound strawberries, washed, stems removed
	1	cup milk
	1	cup whipping cream
	2	tablespoons confectioners' sugar

Serve chilled. Yields 6 servings.

Cranberry Fruit Nut Bread (PCOL)

This is one of my favorites; the inside is white and red, with flecks of gold—appropriate for Brigit. Buy a couple of extra bags of cranberries at Yule and freeze them until Imbolc. Double this recipe using one 12-ounce bag and you get one loaf for you and one for your Imbolc celebration!

Wash, sort, and cut in half	1½	cups fresh or frozen cranberries
Sift together	2	cups flour
	1	cup sugar
	1½	teaspoons baking powder
	1	teaspoon salt
	½	teaspoon baking soda
Cut in	¼	cup butter
Mix together	1	teaspoon grated orange peel
	¾	cup orange juice
	1	egg, well-beaten

Add to flour mixture and mix just to moisten.

| Fold in | ½ | cup chopped pecans |
| | 1½ | cups cranberries |

Turn into greased 9 by 5 by 3-inch loaf pan (even non-stick pans need greasing). Bake at 350 degrees for at least 60 minutes, until the top is golden brown and a toothpick comes out clean. Cool if you can stand the wait, or serve piping hot.

Variation: bake in greased muffin tins for 30 minutes.

Drinks All 'Round!

Ancient Syllabub (A, V)

No one knows if the ancients called this "syllabub," but since both cream and mead, as well as nuts, were available during midwinter, chances are good that they concocted this and enjoyed it as much as we do.

Whip together until stiff   1   cup heavy cream (whipping cream)
                                  ½–⅔   cup mead

Chill for at least an hour, spoon into 4 glasses.

Top with   2   tablespoons hazelnuts, finely ground

Serve cold. Serves 4.

What Else to Drink in Ancient Times?

Unless one lived near a clear spring, water was frequently not a healthy beverage. Adding a percentage of alcoholic beverages to the water not only added flavor, but (unknown to the people) killed the microbeasties that otherwise made them sick.

For historical accuracy, help yourself to any of these (with ale being by far the favorite of the times): ale; hard cider, pear cider; fruit wines (elderberry, apple, plum, and blackberry); other wines (parsnip, parsley, turnip, oak-leaf, cowslip); and of course, mead in all its variations, made at least six months before drinking. Mead is an art unto itself, so we won't try to get into it here; we recommend the recipes in *Mad About Mead* by Pamela Spence (Llewellyn, 1997).

Post-Crusades Version: add wine, although it has never been a competitor for ale, stout, and beer in Ireland.

Mulled Cider or Wine (PCR, V)

Keep a pot simmering all day to scent the house, instead of incense!

In large pot, heat   Apple cider or wine (all red or
                             half red, half white)

Combine (in muslin bag if you don't want to bother with spice bits floating about)

Cinnamon sticks
Cloves, whole
Orange wedges
Allspice (post-Columbus version)
Cardamom (only in wine, not cider)

Keep muslin bag in pot; replenish cider or wine as it is consumed.

Post-Columbus Beverages

To all the other drinks previously mentioned, add cocoa, coffee, and tea. Coffee and tea came from the east, not America, but they arrived at almost the same time as American foods. Rum, gin, and the other distilled liquors appeared in the sixteenth century, but the crowning glory of the distiller's art was whiskey, so have a shot of the best Irish for Lady Brede. And always remember the Irish proverb: "What butter and whiskey won't cure, there's no cure for."

Amber adds: Not everyone "drinks"; a cup of hot tea with lemon or honey is just as satisfying as any of these beverages.

Victorian Syllabub (PCOL, V)

Originally a scullery maid would have beaten this by hand, of course.

Stir together in ceramic or glass bowl

Zest and juice of 3 lemons or 2 oranges
1 cup sherry or white wine
  (depending on personal preference)
¼ cup sugar

Let it sit for at least an hour. Then strain it into a blender and add:

3 cups heavy cream

Blend until thick, chill for an hour, spoon into tall glasses, sprinkle with nutmeg, and serve immediately. Serves 8.

Any combination of cream, wine or wine-based spirits, and a little citrus is entitled to the name "Syllabub." Each cook seems to have had a unique recipe, which could change depending on the ingredients available! For more syllabub recipes, see *Celtic Folklore Cooking* by Joanne Asala (Llewellyn, 1998).

Hot Buttered Rum MMMMix (PCOL, V)

(Thanks to Buck Thompson)

In mixer using dough hook, or by hand, mix	14	ounces whipped unsalted butter
	2	pounds light brown sugar
	1	teaspoon each: cinnamon, nutmeg, ground cloves

Store in refrigerator.

For Hot Buttered Rum:

Combine in mug, stir until mix dissolves	1	heaping tablespoon HBR Mix
	⅔	cup boiling water
Add		Rum to brim

Final Blessings

We thank you all for joining our feast, and leave you with two blessings:

Give thanks to Lady Brede
For meat and bread and mead,
For we are very blessed indeed,
And share with those in need.

—Traditional

And from Bride's Scottish folk:

Some hae meat tha canna eat,
And some hae none that want it.
But we hae meat, and we can eat,
And sae our Bride be thankit.

—Based on a traditional grace

And remember: "The end of a feast is always better than the beginning of a fight."

Conclusion

Outdoors, twilight comes early to the cold land. Long shadows reach across the snow from the leafless boughs of trees, black against the chilly pinks and purples of the sunset. Small tracks show where an animal, perhaps a fox, foraged through the dead leaves at the base of a drift. The fox is gone. High in the deepening sky, a bird beats into the dying breeze; even though it is only a tiny silhouette in the distance, somehow it looks tired and hungry.

February in Northern Europe . . . or for that matter, Minnesota, or Hokkaido in Japan, or the steppes of Siberia. We can be forgiven if we look about us and see only the empty landscapes and the deep, deep cold . . . if we feel our hearts a little frozen, our thoughts touched with gloom. Spring seems very far away. Life seems very far away.

At times like this, the festival reminds us of truths that are hidden like crocuses beneath the snow. It reminds us that the days really are a little longer than they were at Yule . . . that some plants have survived the winter intact, and others are beginning to sprout despite the chilly soil . . . that a few animals are awakening from their long hibernation . . . that already the birds are winging north from their winter feeding grounds.

The festival reminds us of light, and warmth, and new life blossoming; that the Wheel turns—and turning, brings hope. Where there is hope of spring and flowers and warm sunlight, it may be that there is hope for our lives—that beyond the pain and loss and loneliness that come to each human life, there is healing and discovery, love and redemption.

It is about hope. When we embrace the holiday, we embrace hope. When we weave little crosses out of straw, we hope that they will somehow presage luck and prosperity. When we read the old tales of Saint Brigid, we hope that perhaps it really happened that way: that the leper was healed, the king was generous, the fox escaped. When we approach the table filled with succulent food, we hope that there will be plenty of good things for our family to eat until the next harvest.

We hope that life will be good while it lasts, and that when we die, we will discover ourselves moving through a cycle greater than the Wheel of the Year, through death and back to life again.

The season looks sere and bleak, and yet so much is happening. At Eleusis in Greece, celebrants comb the beach by torchlight, little knowing that the Divine Daughter Persephone has begun her journey of return from Hades' dark realm.

Flowers spring up from Brigit's footprints in the snow, as she makes her way through the village to bless your home. Dragons dance in the streets of Chinatown. Farmers offer quiet blessings on the tools of their trade. Japanese lanterns glow in the dusk as friends gather. Somewhere high in the world tree, Woden whispers endearments to the giantess Gerda.

On the fells of Yorkshire, snow flies as a ewe licks a tiny lamb that has just come into the world. At a temple somewhere in the Caribbean, a roomful of Yoruba faithful chant and dance to honor Oya. A priest crosses two lit candles and blesses a parishioner by touching her throat with them. In the American home of a Wiccan couple, their coven gathers to cleanse and bless the house, especially the new nursery. And in a meadow lost in the hills of Thessaly, Pan fingers his pipes and dreams of laughing maidens being chased by goatskin-clad youths.

All these are expressions of hope; and where there is hope, there should be action. The Candlemas sabbat is a turning point, when we lift our eyes from inner remembrance and reflection and begin to envision the season of growth that lies ahead. Envisioning, we move to make it happen. Now is the time for cleansing and purification, for discarding the outworn things of the year past so that we may create room in our lives for the Goddess' new bounty. Now is the time for cleaning the old tools, lighting the new fire, and turning the soil in the garden.

Now is the time for initiation—for releasing who we were, and embracing transformation, rebirth, and new beginnings. It is the time for becoming who we can be, and greeting the new year with our spirits pure and fresh and ready for wonder.

Resources

The Internet

A surprising number of web sites include Imbolg, Candlemas, Brigid, or other subjects related to the holiday. A quick check through the AOL search engine in December 2000 gave us the following numbers of hits for these searches:

	December 2000	September 2001
Brigid	293	328
Brigantia	33	26
Saint Bridget	56	21,095*
Bride	4,164**	
Saint Blaise	28	16,903

* Mostly parish websites, including St. Bridget's Chinese Catholic Center!

**As you might guess, most of these are about weddings, not the goddess, so in September 2001 we searched Brigit instead of Bride: 56.

Candlemas	76	103
Oimelc	21	10
Imbolc	92	116
Imbolg	21	22
Laa'l Breeshey	5	19
Groundhog Day	198	41,266
Chinese New Year	197	1,016,620

Of course you can find even more sources by using more than one search engine, and by entering several different terms or phrases related to the holiday. Don't forget to search with different spelling variations—note that Imbolc had 116 hits, whereas Imbolg had only 22. New sites are being added at a great rate, so the number of sites will only grow with time.

Some Brigid-oriented websites worth visiting include "Brighid," "Brighid's Eternal Flame," "Brigit at the Shrine of the Forgotten Goddesses," "Full Moon Dreams," and "The Hearth." If you want to spend the rest of your life searching, ixquick came up with 50,640 matches for Brigid.

Organizations

Brighid's Academy of Healing Arts: School of Herbalism, Celtic Spirituality & Holistic Healing, 22711 Highway 36, Cheshire, OR 97419. Tel. 541-998-7986. Website: www.celtic.net/brighid.

The Chalice Center, P.O. Box 3839, Carmel, CA 93921. E-mail: office@chalicecenter.com.

Daughters of the Flame c/o #14-2320 Woodland Drive, Vancouver, B.C. V5N 3P2, Canada. E-mail: spinkus@interchange.ubc.ca. "On Imbolc, 1993, the D.O.F. lit a fire in honor of the Goddess Brigit, modeled after the perpetual fire which once burned in Kildare. We share the task of tending the flame, on a twenty-day rotation; each woman tends the fire in her own way, so that it is a solitary devotion linked to the devotions of a larger group. On the twentieth day the Goddess Herself keeps the flame alive. Instead of burning in one grove, temple, or monastery, it burns on personal altars, desks, and picnic tables in Canada, Australia, New Zealand, England, and the United States. . . ." There are three cells of nineteen shifts each. The DOF publishes a newsletter, has a reading list/library, and sponsors a Prayer Help-Line. Website: http://www.madstone.com/DaughtersoftheFlame.

Ord Brighideach. "An order of flame-keepers engaged in tending Her flame within a traditional twenty-day cycle and in devotional work to the goddess Brighid . . . an order of druids who seek to find a bridge between pagan, christian and all nonharmful spiritual loyalties. Brighid, as goddess of the Gaels and saint of the Christians, is the matron of this clan." Has cells with women only, men only, and co-ed. Website: http://members.aol.com/gmkkh/brighid/ob.html.

More OB websites can be found using a meta search engine like ixquick and search words "Ord Brighideach."

Statuary

Sacred Source. This outlet has statues of Brigid and many other deities. Website: www.sacredsource.com.

Small Anvils

Tandy Leather has small anvils that weigh just two pounds and are about 4½-inches long by 2-inches wide, at their stores nationwide. Or they can be ordered from www.TandyLeather.com, product number 40500. Phone: 1-888-890-1611.

Publications

Brigid of the Gael by Conrad Bladey. Includes both early historical primary references, poems, hymns, stories about the saint, folk customs, recipes for celebrating her holy day, and an extensive bibliography. 154 pages, $19.00, available from the same source listed above. Order form online at http://members.nbci.com/_XMCM/bladocelt/bripub.html.

The Good Saint Brigid of Kildare by Conrad Bladey. A short (20 pages) introduction to the Irish saint. $3.75 from Conrad Bladey, P.O. Box 268, Linthicum, Maryland 21090 USA.

The Triple Flame, newsletter and network entirely devoted to Brighid. Faerin NaFior, editor. P.O. Box 10740, Pensacola, FL 32524-0740. Back issues available. Submissions welcome. (via DF website)

Bibliography

"The Annals of the Four Masters," Milesian Genealogies, in "A Timeline of Irish History," Clannada na Gadelica website.

Bain, Iain. *Celtic Knotwork.* New York: Sterling Publishing Co., 1986.

Bain, George. *Celtic Art: the Methods of Construction.* New York: Dover Publications, 1973.

Beane, William and William Doty, eds. *Myths, Rites, Symbols: A Mircea Eliade Reader.* New York: Harper Colophon, 1975.

Bladey, Conrad. "Proverbs of Ireland," Conrad Bladey's Irish Studies Pages website.

Buckland, Raymond. *Practical Color Magick.* St. Paul: Llewellyn, 1983.

Cambrensis, Gerald. *The History and Topography of Ireland*, John J. O'Meara, trans. Portlaoise: Dolmen Press, 1982.

Cambrensis, Giraldus. *Topographia Hibernie*, trans. Philip Freeman, quoted in *The Celtic Heroic Age, Literary Sources for Ancient Celtic Europe and Early Ireland and Wales,* Ed. John Koch, Malden Mass.: Celtic Studies Publications, 1995; on Brigit's Forge website.

Campanelli, Pauline. *Ancient Ways: Reclaiming Pagan Traditions.* St. Paul: Llewellyn Publications, 1991.

———. *The Wheel of the Year.* St. Paul: Llewellyn Publications, 1990.

Carmichael, Alexander. *Carmina Gadelica.* Edinburgh: Floris Press, 1992.

Catholic Encyclopedia, Volume II, Robert Appleton Company, 1907. Online.

Condren, Mary. *The Serpent and the Goddess: Women, Religion, and Power in Celtic Ireland.* San Francisco: HarperSanFrancisco, 1989.

Conway, D. J. *Magick of the Gods and Goddesses.* St. Paul: Llewellyn Publications, 1993.

Reader's Digest. *Crafts and Hobbies*. Pleasantville, New York: Reader's Digest Assn., Inc., 1979.

The Crescent, issue 2000, Re-Formed Congregation of the Goddess, Madison, WI, 2000.

Cunningham, Scott. *The Magic of Incense, Oils, and Brews*. St. Paul: Llewellyn Publications, 1986.

Davis, Courtney. *Celtic Borders and Decoration*. London: Blandford, 1992.

Deegan, Tina. "Flora and Fauna Associated with Brighid" and "Historical Background On The 'Exalted One'." Shrine of the Goddess Brighid website.

Donncha, Dennis King. "Old Irish Poem" in e-mail to Branfionn NicGrioghair, "Brighid, Bright Goddess of the Gael" in IMBAS website.

Dunwich, Gerina. *The Magick of Candle Burning*. New York: Citadel Press, 1989.

Farrar, Janet and Stewart. *Eight Sabbats for Witches*. London: Robert Hale, 1981.

"February 1: Imbolc." Chalice Center website.

Fitzjohn, Sue, et al. *Festivals Together, A Guide to Multi-Cultural Celebration*. Stroud, Gloucestershire, UK: Hawthorn Press, 1993.

"Fomorians," Encyclopedia Mythica website.

Fox, Selena. "Candlemas Customs and Lore," Circle Sanctuary website.

Gibson, Walter B. and Litzka R. *The Complete Illustrated Book of Divination and Prophecy*. London: Souvenir Press, 1973.

Gimbutas, Marija. *The Goddesses and Gods of Old Europe, 6500–3500 BC, Myths and Cult Images*. Berkeley and Los Angeles: University of California Press, 1982.

Green, Marian. *A Calendar of Festivals: Traditional Celebrations, Songs, Seasonal Recipes & things to Make*. Shaftesbury, Dorset: Element, 1991.

Green, Miranda. *Celtic Goddesses, Warriors, Virgins and Mothers*. George Braziller Inc., 1995.

_____. *The World of the Druids*. London: Thames and Hudson, 1997.

Gregory, Lady Augusta. *A Book of Saints and Wonders Put Down Here by Lady Gregory According to the Old Writings and the Memory of the People of Ireland*. London: John Murray, 1907. Quoted on several websites noted below.

Grimassi, Raven. *Encyclopedia of Wicca & Witchcraft*. St. Paul: Llewellyn Publications, 2000.

K, Amber. *Covencraft: Witchcraft for Three or More*. St. Paul: Llewellyn Publications, 1998.

Lafferty, Ann. "Imbolc." *EarthSpirit* newsletter, Winter 1994.

Lord, Jarman. "The Anglo-Saxon Year Division," files of Amber K; original publication source unknown.

MacDonald, L. "Celtic Folklore: The People of the Mounds—Articles on the Sidhe," *Dalriada Magazine,* 1993, quoted on ShadowNet website, November 1995, Issue 1.

Macleod, Fiona (William Sharp). *Winged Destiny: Studies in the Spiritual History of the Gael.* London: William Heinemann, 1910 (see website).

Manning-Sanders, Ruth (compiler). *Festivals.* New York: E. P. Dutton, 1973.

McCoy, Edain. *The Sabbats.* St. Paul: Llewellyn Publications, 1994.

McGarry , Mary (compiler). *Great Folk Tales of Old Ireland.* New York: Bell Publishing, 1972.

Monaghan, Patricia. *The New Book of Goddesses & Heroines.* St. Paul: Llewellyn Publications, 1997 (3rd edition).

Morwyn. *Witch's Brew.* Atglen, Penn.: Whitford Press, 1995.

Murray, Liz and Colin. *The Celtic Tree Oracle.* New York: St. Martin's Press, 1988.

The New Columbia Encyclopedia. New York: Columbia University Press, 1975.

Newman, Thelma R. *Creative Candlemaking.* New York: Crown Publishers, Inc., 1972.

NicGrioghair, Branfionn. "Brighid, Bright Goddess of the Gael" in IMBAS website.

Ó Cáthain, Séamas. *The Festival of Brigit.* Dublin: DBA Publications, 1995, in Chalice Center website.

O'Donovan, John, trans. *The Martyrology of Donegal, A Calendar of the Saints of Ireland.* Dublin, The Irish Archaeological and Celtic Society, 1864. (Original: Michael O'Clery, compiler, Donegal, April 19, 1630). Quoted in several websites.

O'Neill, Helen. "Bridget's Legacy," The Associated Press, 1998.

RavenWolf, Silver. *To Ride a Silver Broomstick: New Generation Witchcraft.* St. Paul: Llewellyn Publications, 1994.

Rogers, Barbara Radcliffe. *Yankee Home Crafts.* Dublin, New Hamp.: Yankee, Inc., 1979.

Ryall, Rhiannon. *West Country Wicca.* Custer Wash.: Phoenix Publishing, 1989.

Sabrina, Lady. *Exploring Wicca.* Franklin Lakes, New Jersey: New Page, 2000.

"San Diego's Chinese Community Home Page," *San Diego Magazine* website.

"Scandinavian Dublin," www.indiao.ie/~kfinlay/ossory/ossory1.htm.

Shepler, John. "It's Groundhog Day and the Forecast is . . . ," John Shepler's Writing in a Positive Light website.

Spindler, Lisa, "Brigid," Encyclopedia Mythica website.

Starhawk. *The Spiral Dance: A Rebirth of the Ancient Religion of the Great Goddess*. 10th Anniversary ed. HarperSanFrancisco, 1989.

Stokes, Whitley, trans. *Lives of Saints from the Book of Lismore*. Oxford, 1890. Quoted in several websites.

The Sweetgrass Times, Winter 1998-9, Vol. 1 No. 1. At Sweetgrass website.

Uyldert, Mellie. *The Magic of Precious Stones*. Wellingborough, Northamptonshire: Turnstone Press, Unlimited, 1981.

Valiente, Doreen. *ABC of Witchcraft*. New York: St. Martin's Press, 1973.

———. *Witchcraft for Tomorrow*. New York: St. Martin's Press, 1978.

Walker, Barbara G. *The Woman's Encyclopedia of Myths and Secrets*. San Francisco: Harper & Row, 1983.

Webster's Encyclopedic Unabridged Dictionary of the English Language. New York: Random House Value Publishing, 1996.

Whitcomb, Bill. *The Magician's Companio*n. St. Paul: Llewellyn Publications, 1993.

Wolf, Casey. "Sisters of the Flame." Quoted in Daughters of the Flame website.

Wood, Hilaire. "Brigit the Saint" on Brigit's Forge website.

Zell, Morning Glory, Unnamed article in *AMARGI*, Vol. I No. 3, Feb. 1st 1989. Quoted in Daughters of the Flame website.

Websites

ADF Neopagan Druidism. www.adf.org (Ár nDraíocht Féin)

Brighid's Academy of Healing Arts website

Brighid.hypermart.net/aboutbrighid.html

Brigit's Forge website. www.brigitsforge.co.uk/index.html

Catholic Information Network website. http://www.cin.org/saints/bridget/html

Catholic Online website. www.catholic.org/saints/saints/brigidireland.html

Chalice Center website. www.chalicecenter.com/imbolc.htm

China website: www.educ.UVIC.ca/faculty/mroth/438/CHINA/chinese

Circle Sanctuary website. www.circlesanctuary.org/pholidays/CandlemasCustomsLore.html

Clannada na Gadelica website. www.clannada.org

Collected Works of Fiona Macleod (William Sharp) website
    http://www.sundown.pair.com/SundownShores/webbklst.htm

Conrad Bladey's Irish Studies Pages website
    www.ncf.carleton.ca/~bj333/HomePage.proverbs.html

Daughters of the Flame website. www.madstone.com/Daughters oftheFlame

Encyclopedia Mythica website. www.pantheon.org/mythica/articles/f/fomorians.html

For All the Saints website. http://users.erols.com/saintpat/ss/0201.htm#bng
    www.garden.com (Super candles!)

Imbas website. http://www.imbas.org/brighid.htm

John Shepler's Writing in a Positive Light website
    http://www.execpc.com/shepler/groundhog

Ord Brighideach website. http://members.aol.com/gmkkh/brighid/ob/htm

"San Diego's Chinese Community Home Page," *San Diego Magazine* website
    www.sandiego-online.com/forums/chinese/htmls

"Scandinavian Dublin," www.indiao.ie/~kfinlay/ossory/ossory1.htm

ShadowNet website. www.tO.or.at/~dkollmer/SN/sidhe.htm

Shrine of the Goddess Brighid website, http://homepages.jireh.co.uk/~fealcen/brigit.htm

Martha Stewart website. www.marthastewart.com

The Sweetgrass Times. www.users.qwest.net/~ladybear/SGwinter98.htm

Feast Bibliography

Asala, Joanne. *Celtic Folklore Cooking.* St. Paul: Llewellyn Publications, 1998.

Bailey, Adrian. *The Blessings of Bread.* New York and London: Paddington Press, Ltd., 1975.

Bailey, Adrian. *The Cooking of the British Isles. Foods of the World.* New York: Time-Life Books, 1969, 1975.

Ettinger, John. *Cooking With Herbs.* Rocklin, Calif.: Prima Publishing, 1996.

Foster, Nelson, and Linda S. Cordell. *Chilies to Chocolate.* Tucson: University of Arizona Press, 1992.

Goddard, Winifred. *How to Cook Fish and Game.* Christchurch, New Zealand: Whitcomb and Tombs, 1967.

Jacob, H. E. *Six Thousand Years of Bread.* Republished. New York: The Lyons Press, 1997.

Katzen, Mollie. *Moosewood Cookbook.* Berkeley: Ten Speed Press, 1977.

Kinsella, Mary. *An Irish Farmhouse Cookbook.* Appletree Press, 1983.

Nearing, Helen. *Simple Food for the Good Life.* Walpole, New Hamp.: Stillpoint Publishing, 1980.

Pearson, Lu Emily. *Elizabethans at Home.* Stanford, Calif.: Stanford University Press, 1957.

Rombauer, Irma, and Marion Rombauer Becker. *The Joy of Cooking.* Indianapolis and New York: Bobbs-Merrill, 1975.

Root, Waverly. *Food.* New York: Simon & Schuster, 1980.

Ryall, Rhiannon. *West Country Wicca.* Custer, Wash.: Phoenix Publishing, 1989.

Tannahill, Reay. *Food in History.* New York: Three Rivers Press, 1988.

Viola, Herman J. and Carolyn Margolis. *Seeds of Change.* Washington, D.C.: Smithsonian Institution, 1991.

Index

☽ REACH FOR THE MOON

Llewellyn publishes hundreds of books on your favorite subjects! To get these exciting books, including the ones on the following pages, check your local bookstore or order them directly from Llewellyn.

Order by Phone
- Call toll-free within the U.S. and Canada, 1-800-THE MOON
- In Minnesota, call (651) 291-1970
- We accept VISA, MasterCard, and American Express

Order by Mail
- Send the full price of your order (MN residents add 7% sales tax) in U.S. funds, plus postage & handling to:

  Llewellyn Worldwide
  P.O. Box 64383, Dept. 0-7387-0079-7
  St. Paul, MN 55164–0383, U.S.A.

Postage & Handling
- **Standard** (U.S., Mexico, & Canada)

If your order is:
  $20.00 or under, add $5.00
  $20.01–$100.00, add $6.00
  Over $100, shipping is free
(Continental U.S. orders ship UPS. AK, HI, PR, & P.O. Boxes ship USPS 1st class. Mex. & Can. ship PMB.)

- **Second Day Air** (Continental U.S. only): $10.00 for one book + $1.00 per each additional book
- **Express** (AK, HI, & PR only) [Not available for P.O. Box delivery. For street address delivery only.]: $15.00 for one book + $1.00 per each additional book
- **International Surface Mail:** Add $1.00 per item
- **International Airmail:** Books—Add the retail price of each item; Non-book items—Add $5.00 per item

Please allow 4–6 weeks for delivery on all orders.
Postage and handling rates subject to change.

Discounts
We offer a 20% discount to group leaders or agents. You must order a minimum of 5 copies of the same book to get our special quantity price.

Free Catalog
Get a free copy of our color catalog, *New Worlds of Mind and Spirit*. Subscribe for just $10.00 in the United States and Canada ($30.00 overseas, airmail).

Visit our website at www.llewellyn.com for more information.

BELTANE
Springtime Rituals, Lore & Celebration

Raven Grimassi

Beltane examines the ancient pagan origins of May Day festivals that thrived up to the end of the nineteenth century. Explore the evolution of the May Pole and various folklore characters connected to May Day celebrations. Discover the influences of ancient Greek and Roman religions on May themes arising in the Celtic cultures of continental Europe and the British Isles.

Beltane includes arts and craft projects, recipes for celebratory meals, and several spells related to the May themes of growth and gain. There is also a Beltane ritual for both solitary and group practitioners.

This well-researched book corrects many of the common misconceptions associated with May Day. It will help the reader more fully appreciate the spirituality and connection to Nature that are intimate elements of May Day celebrations.

- Learn the inner meanings of May Day celebrations

- Make an authentic May Pole centerpiece for your Beltane festivities

- Cast spells for gain and success in harmony with the season of growth

- Perform a May Day ritual of alignment with the forces of Nature

- Explore fairy lore and flower lore dating back to nineteenth-century sources

1-56718-283-6, 192 pp., 7½ x 9⅛, illus.   **$14.95**

YULE
A Celebration of Light and Warmth

Dorothy Morrison

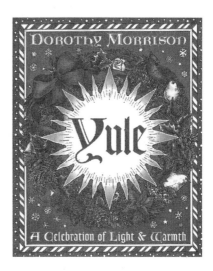

The "holidays": some call them Christmas or Hanukkah, others know them as Los Posadas or Ta Dhiu. Still others celebrate Winter Solstice or Yule. They are a time for reflection, resolution, and renewal. Whatever our beliefs, the holidays provide us with rituals to celebrate the balance of light and dark, and for welcoming the healing powers of warmth back into our world.

Jam packed with more than sixty spells, invocations, and rituals, *Yule* guides you through the magic of the season. Traveling its realm will bring back the joy you felt as a child—the spirit of warmth and good will that lit the long winter nights. Discover the origin of the eight tiny reindeer, brew up some Yuletide coffee, and learn ways to create your own holiday traditions and crafts based on celebrations from a variety of countries and beliefs.

1-56718-496-0, 216 pp., 7½ x 9⅛, 56 illus. $14.95

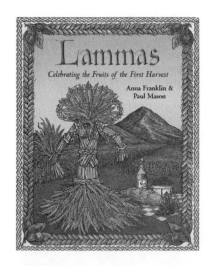

LAMMAS
Celebrating the Fruits of the First Harvest

Anna Franklin and Paul Mason

The most obscure of the witches' festivals.
Although it has an ancient and fascinating history, Lammas (or Lughnasa) is now one of the most obscure of the eight festivals of the witches' Wheel of the Year. Celebrated in early August to mark the beginning of harvest, the name comes from the Irish Gaelic násad (games) of Lugh (a leading Celtic deity and hero).

Lammas describes the origins of the festival and compares similar festivals around the world, including Celtic, Norse, Egyptian, Russian, English, and Native American. You will find practical advice on how to celebrate the festival, themes to explore, recipes, incense, spells, traditional types of divination, and several full rituals, including a traditional witch ritual never before published.

- Discover the ancient and mysterious festival of Lammas/Lughnasa and its origins

- Explore harvest customs and witness their power today

- Learn the ancient magic practiced at Lammas

- Try out traditional recipes for food, wine, herb teas, and sweets

- Make incense to celebrate the season and invoke its powers

- Honor the gods and goddesses of Lammas

0-7387-0094-0, 284 pp., 7½ x 9⅛, illus. $17.95

To Order, Call 1-800-THE MOON
Prices subject to change without notice